# Making Connections

Full details of all the books in this series and of all our other publications can be found on http://www.multilingual-matters.com, or by writing to Multilingual Matters, St Nicholas House, 31-34 High Street, Bristol, BS1 2AW, UK.

# Making Connections

A Practical Guide to Online Intercultural Exchanges

**John Corbett, Hugo Dart and Bruno Lima**

**MULTILINGUAL MATTERS**
Bristol • Jackson

DOI https://doi.org/10.21832/CORBET2651
Library of Congress Cataloging in Publication Data
Names: Corbett, John, author. | Dart, Hugo, author. | Lima, Bruno, author.
Title: Making Connections: A Practical Guide to Online Intercultural Exchanges/
   John Corbett, Hugo Dart and Bruno Lima.
Description: Bristol; Jackson: Multilingual Matters, [2023] |
   Includes bibliographical references and index. | Summary: "This book is a
   practical, down-to-earth guide for language teachers interested in
   running online intercultural exchanges. It is informed by the latest
   research on language teaching and intercultural telecollaborations, and
   situated in the reality of classrooms around the world"– Provided by publisher.
Identifiers: LCCN 2023024623 (print) | LCCN 2023024624 (ebook)|
ISBN 9781800412651 (hardback; alk. paper) | ISBN 9781800412644 (paperback;
   alk. paper) | ISBN 9781800412675 (epub) | ISBN 9781800412668 (pdf)
Subjects: LCSH: Language and languages–Study and teaching. | Intercultural
   communication–Study and teaching. | Internet in education. | Language and
   languages–Study and teaching–Computer network resources.
Classification: LCC P53.45 .C67 2023 (print) | LCC P53.45 (ebook) |
   DDC 418.0078/5–dc23/eng/20230707
LC record available at https://lccn.loc.gov/2023024623
LC ebook record available at https://lccn.loc.gov/2023024624

British Library Cataloguing in Publication Data
A catalogue entry for this book is available from the British Library.

ISBN-13: 978-1-80041-265-1 (hbk)
ISBN-13: 978-1-80041-264-4 (pbk)

**Multilingual Matters**
UK: St Nicholas House, 31-34 High Street, Bristol, BS1 2AW, UK.
USA: Ingram, Jackson, TN, USA.

Website: www.multilingual-matters.com
Twitter: Multi_Ling_Mat
Facebook: https://www.facebook.com/multilingualmatters
Blog: www.channelviewpublications.wordpress.com

The policy of Multilingual Matters/Channel View Publications is to use papers
that are natural, renewable and recyclable products, made from wood grown in
sustainable forests. In the manufacturing process of our books, and to further
support our policy, preference is given to printers that have FSC and PEFC Chain
of Custody certification. The FSC and/or PEFC logos will appear on those books
where full certification has been granted to the printer concerned.

Typeset by Deanta Global Publishing Services, Chennai, India.

# Contents

# Acknowledgements

Books conventionally include a dedication to those without whom the volume would never have seen the light of day; in our case, we are certainly conscious of the extent of our debt to many, many people whose support and active contributions have been crucial to the writing of this guide. We are indebted, first, to our fellow organisers and instructors who have over the past 25 years been involved in numerous iterations of the online intercultural exchanges that are the basis for the book, principally Wendy Anderson, Andrea Assenti del Rio, Adriana Aquino, Noriko Isihara, Karolina Ísio-Kurpińska, Clarissa Jordão, Peih-ying Lu, Carole MacDiarmid, Julia Menard-Warwick, Rebecca Moura, Nahla Nassar, Janaína Oliveira, Alison Phipps, Malila Prado, Colin Reilly, Krysia Rubiec, Mati Segovia and Erick Tristão. They have been thoughtful and generous partners and collaborators. Over the past few decades, hundreds of participants in the projects have interacted online, giving their consent in advance for our use of their exchanges for the purposes of teaching and research. We are immensely grateful to you all. We have benefited from institutional support over the years from the University of Glasgow, the University of Macau, BNU-HKBU United International College (UIC), the Universidade Federal do Rio Grande do Norte (UFRN), the Instituto Federal de Educação, Ciência e Tecnologia do Rio Grande do Norte (IFRN) and the Instituto Brasil-Estados Unidos (IBEU-RJ). The Norwich Institute for Language Education (NILE) has provided outstanding mentorship and enduring professional friendships. We are also indebted to the anonymous reviewers of this volume for their insights, corrections and advice. The remaining flaws are, naturally, our responsibility. We thank the peerless team at Multilingual Matters for their enthusiasm for this project, and their patience in waiting for the final manuscript to appear. The three authors of this book originally met face-to-face at a BRAZ-TESOL conference, and the BRAZ-TESOL community, especially the Intercultural Language Education Special Interest Group (ILE SIG), has also been an essential sounding board for many of the ideas that are formulated in this volume. Finally, colleagues, friends and family remain a constant inspiration, and a source of comfort and love. Our thanks go particularly to Augusta Alves, Olivia Dart, Rogerio Dart, Samantha Dart, Leonardo Lima, Uwe Pohl, Sandra Saito, Cristina de Souza and Regina Taam (1949–2023).

# 1 Introducing Online Intercultural Exchanges

This book aims to be a useful and practical guide for organisers and instructors who wish to establish and run online intercultural exchanges for language learners. While it is informed by theories of language education and communication, some of which are referred to explicitly, its purpose is not so much to survey or discuss those theories as to give readers hands-on advice on setting up and running an online intercultural exchange. We assume that our readers have no previous experience of running such exchanges, and so we attend to the basics: finding suitable partners, choosing a digital platform, agreeing goals and addressing issues of ethics and security. We consider the kinds of task that organisers and instructors might invite participants in the exchange to do, from ice-breakers to more extensive intercultural language activities. We pay due attention to the important issues of how participants in an exchange create a virtual identity, and how they establish rapport with fellow members of the online community. We offer advice on dealing with any problems that may arise during an exchange. Finally, we consider issues around the assessment of the performance of participants in an online exchange, the evaluation of the exchange as a whole and the use of such a project in action research, perhaps towards a graduate degree. While the nature of online intercultural exchanges varies considerably in different contexts, we hope that our collective experience of developing, running and writing about such exchanges will afford the reader useful advice and insights into their own developing practices.

Although the same people might assume a number of roles in an online exchange, we distinguish among *organisers* who set up an exchange, *instructors* who run it on a day-to-day basis and the *participants* who join the community as a means of enhancing their linguistic and cultural competences. This volume, then, addresses the everyday issues that organisers and instructors must face when setting up and monitoring an online intercultural exchange, or telecollaboration. While our focus is steadfastly on the practical, we also believe that if organisers and instructors are going to develop effective online *intercultural* exchanges, they will also benefit from a framework that helps them to reflect on the

1

nature of interculturality and its role in language pedagogy. This chapter, then, offers readers such a framework. We review the nature of the online intercultural exchange, we invite readers to reflect on the nature of interculturality and we consider, briefly, the role of interculturality in education.

## Online Intercultural Exchanges

Online intercultural exchanges have grown in tandem with the technological revolution sparked by the spread of computer-mediated communication. In an overview of online intercultural exchanges, O'Dowd (2012) observes that interest in online interactions as a tool for teaching language and culture surged in popularity from the 1990s onwards. In a resource book that presents a number of pedagogical tasks designed primarily for online intercultural exchanges, Corbett (2010) states that:

> Computer-mediated communication has given a whole new impetus to the integration of culture-learning with language learning. Many teachers have consequently taken the opportunity to set up collaborative online partnerships with other teachers and learners of English worldwide. (Corbett, 2010: 11)

O'Dowd (2012: 35) refers to such partnerships as 'telecollaborations' and describes them as 'an intercultural approach to language teaching mediated by the internet'. Alluding to their variety, he writes of 'constellations of task design and sequencing'. It is worth taking time to consider some of the formats and options that face organisers and instructors as they begin to think about designing a telecollaboration.

One of the first decisions to be made concerns choice of language or languages. Some exchanges invite participants in the online community to use a number of the different languages at their disposal. For example, Ware and Kramsch (2005: 203) describe telecollaboration as 'a technologically-mediated cultural and linguistic exchange in which learners write to one another in both their native and target language'. Other educators, such as Ware (2005) and Souza (2003), also regard the systematic exchange of messages in two languages as a basic, defining characteristic of telecollaborative partnerships.

Although he acknowledges the possibility of using two or more languages in telecollaborations, O'Dowd (2012: 342) does not see this as a defining feature. He describes telecollaboration simply as 'the application of online communication tools to bring together classes of language learners in geographically distant locations to develop their foreign language skills and intercultural competence through collaborative tasks and project work'. While in some telecollaborations, then, participants use two or more languages (their own and the target languages) to communicate with partners, other exchanges involve the use of a single lingua franca, such as English.

The definition of a telecollaboration adopted by the authors of this book is also relatively simple: we assume that geographically distant participants use the internet to become partners in addressing a shared set of tasks for the purpose of improving their competence in a shared language or shared languages. The computer-mediated communication in the online community may be asynchronous (i.e. participants post messages and these are responded to over time) or synchronous (i.e. participants interact 'live' in real time). Whatever the format, an online *intercultural* exchange anticipates that participants in the community will do more than enhance their purely linguistic competence; there will also be an intercultural component to their learning. If organisers and instructors of telecollaborations are to address the intercultural aspects of this learning effectively, they need to have a clear idea of what they understand by interculturality. They also need to consider how online exchanges can promote the development of interculturality.

## The Nature of Interculturality

By engaging in a series of online interactions with partners from diverse backgrounds, we assume that participants in telecollaborations are required to bring into play resources of knowledge and skill that can be described as 'intercultural'. Numerous educators have attempted to describe the knowledge and skills that are at stake in intercultural communication (e.g. Byram, 1997, 2008; Corbett, 2003, 2022) and they are most fully expressed in two lengthy documents that articulate the *Common European Framework of Reference for Languages: Learning, Teaching, Assessment* (CEFR; Council of Europe, 2001; North *et al.*, 2018). The introduction to the CEFR states that:

> in an intercultural approach, it is a central objective of language learning to promote the favourable development of the learner's whole personality and sense of identity to the enriching experience of otherness in language and culture. (Council of Europe, 2001: 1)

Later formulations of intercultural communicative competence focus less on enrichment and more on the attitudes and skills necessary for mediating between different perspectives, attitudes, beliefs and goals (cf. Corbett, 2021).

The notion of intercultural communicative competence, then, has developed over time and there are different, sometimes contested, ways of conceptualising it (e.g. Byram, 1997, 2008; Corbett, 2022; Deardoff, 2009; Dervin & Gross, 2016). In general, however, all the approaches to the teaching of language that have the fostering of interculturality as a primary goal consider language as a means of exploration and mediation in situations where cultural difference is encountered and so conflicts potentially occur. An intercultural approach to language education thus encourages the development of qualities such as open-minded curiosity, empathy and respect for others, alongside linguistic skills. In addition to qualities that promote resilience in situations where cultures clash, an intercultural approach should stimulate learners to discover and reflect on their own culture as a means to better understand the world immediately around them.

Byram (1997, 2008) presents three communicative contexts in which intercultural competence is likely to be required:

- Communication between people of different languages and countries, in which one of the speakers is a native speaker of the language in use.
- Communication between people of different languages and countries where the language in common use is a lingua franca.
- Communication between people of the same country, but of different languages, in which one of them is a native speaker of the language in use.

Online intercultural exchanges typically involve either the first or the second of the aforementioned contexts. The authors of the present volume have been involved, on different occasions, with participants from Argentina, Brazil, Britain, China, Cyprus, Greece, Japan, Palestine, Poland, Macao, Taiwan and the United States, all of whom have come together to discuss, in English, aspects of their cultures and everyday lives. However, these 'national' groupings mask underlying diversity: a group based in Glasgow included exchange students from Europe, for example, and several exchanges involved participants from geographically and socially diverse parts of Brazil, and linguistically distinct groups in China.

The designers of online intercultural exchanges among participants from these diverse contexts must address issues beyond the simple exchange of information on topics such as food, festivals and folklore. Again, a broadly accepted model of intercultural communicative competence (e.g. Byram, 1997, 2008) has the advantage of specifying sets of knowledge, skills and attitude that can serve as shared goals for organisers, instructors and learners. These can be summarised as follows:

- Attitudes: Being curious and open to suspending disbelief regarding other cultures and beliefs about one's own culture.
- Knowledge: Knowing the products and practices of a social group in their own country and in the interlocutor's country, in addition to general principles of social interaction.

- Interpretation and relationship skills: Interpreting a document or event from another culture, explaining it and relating it to documents and events in one's own culture.
- Discovery and interaction skills: Acquiring knowledge of a culture and knowing how to operate it under the circumstances of real-time communication.
- Critical cultural awareness and political education: Critically and judiciously evaluate the practices and products of one's own and the interlocutor's culture.

In light of these skills and qualities, it is possible to say that interculturality involves the perception of communication as a democratic act of social interaction and the acknowledgement of respect for other individuals and groups. In an educational context, interculturality implies that participants ideally become agents of change, that is, actors working for social transformation, occupying a space between cultures, conventional meanings and languages.

The ideal consequence, then, of developing interculturality is the formation of 'global citizens' (Guilherme, 2002). Similarly, Byram (2008) presents education for intercultural citizenship as a politically engaged teaching of languages, as a response to globalisation. More specifically,

> Education for intercultural citizenship [...] deliberately facilitates or creates experiences where the qualities of being intercultural are developed. It focuses on experiences that are political, in the sense of working together with people of other groups to achieve an agreed purpose. Because of this focus, education for intercultural citizenship expects to create change in the individual, to promote their learning. (Byram, 2008: 187)

When designing an online intercultural exchange, then, the organisers and instructors might consider if or how the activities support the development of intercultural communicative competence and the formation of global citizenship. The intent is to create experiences that require collaboration to achieve agreed goals. In the process of achieving these goals, individuals become aware of and mediate attitudes, beliefs and ways of being that are potentially transformative.

There are, as we shall see, many possible ways to develop activities to support these aspirations. The participants in online exchanges will also have their own ideas about global citizenship. For example, two of the present authors were involved in establishing an online exchange in which students from Natal in Brazil and Gaza in Palestine might meet and use the English language creatively to explore their respective conditions of occupation and economic marginalisation. While this happened to some extent, once the participants realised that both cities lie on the coast, they became equally interested in each other's attitudes towards beach culture. They found an unexpected commonality in their mutual interest in beach life (Alareer *et al.*, 2022). As Anderson and Corbett (2015) observe, while organisers can certainly establish an exchange designed explicitly to address urgent issues of global concern and social justice, simply chatting online to someone from a diverse background about everyday life can develop aspects of intercultural competence. The key issue is whether or not the telecollaboration promotes intercultural dialogue.

## Intercultural Dialogue

The concept of intercultural dialogue draws on the work of cultural theorist, Homi Bhabha (1994). Bhabha envisaged, as a potential outcome of intercultural dialogue, participants' mutual understanding of irreducible differences in their attitudes and beliefs, while continuing to acknowledge the possibility of conciliation. It follows from Bhabha's insights that the role of online intercultural exchanges should be to provide participants with opportunities for active engagement in collecting information about different ways of being. The exchange should also encourage reflection and critical thinking about learners' own subjectivities and cultural contexts. Thus, according to Tomaél and Marteleto (2006), the first step would be to gather from participants information that comprises different views of the world. It is this information that then provides the basis for the expression of different cultural representations and values. In the words of Cope and Kalantzis (2000: 18):

> every classroom will inevitably reconfigure the relationships of local and global difference that are now so critical. To be relevant, learning processes need to recruit [...] interests, intentions, commitments and purposes that students bring to learning.

Cope and Kalantzis (2000) point out that tensions between the local and the global can be made manifest in classroom activities that will motivate learners, and that problematising these tensions is important in fostering intercultural awareness and actualising the potential for conciliation that Bhabha (1994) foresaw.

For example, learners from different parts of the world can be prompted to discuss among themselves the reasons why some people from their different locations might choose to wait in line for hours, sometimes even days, just to purchase the latest-generation smartphone of a certain brand. Such discussions might lead to the realisation that such consumers not only desire access to all the functions the new device brings, but they also crave whatever symbolic value is attached to the product. Learners might then be prompted to consider how corporate marketing campaigns shape discourses, on a global scale, to instigate in consumers a sense of belonging to a caste of people who can afford the newest cell phone. At the same time, learners might relate the shared global aspiration to diverse local conditions by exploring among themselves the variation in the number of hours an individual in each locality would need to work in order to be able to buy the smartphone in question. The activity can easily be adapted to other prestige consumer items, such as sneakers.

This is only one kind of simple dialogic activity that can be used in exchanges to attain the outcomes proposed by theorists and educators, from Bhabha to Cope and Kalantzis, and which are reflected in the activities suggested in later chapters of this volume. Through a series of dialogues, mediated by devices linked to the internet, learners from diverse places and backgrounds can be prompted, directly or indirectly, to approach aspects of their subjectivities, such as gender identity, sexual orientation, social class, ethnicity, generation and geographical origin. By engaging in such dialogues and reflecting on the outcome, they will enhance their intercultural competence.

## Developing Intercultural Competence through Telecollaborations

The use of online exchanges in the development of interculturality involves setting tasks that will develop the ability to learn reflectively, learn autonomously, apply critical cultural awareness and develop a personal stake in the learning process. We consider these briefly in turn.

### A virtual 'third space'

We have already mentioned the key elements of intercultural communicative competence. Belz and Thorne (2006: x) argue that telecollaboration can be a set of practices that function 'in a supportive environment and in pedagogically sound ways' to develop these elements. There are many case studies and discussions of particular online exchanges (e.g. the chapters in O'Dowd [2007] and Potolia and Derivry-Plard [2023]), and O'Dowd and Lewis (2016) also offer a systematic review of policies and practices used in intercultural telecollaborations.

Key to many online intercultural exchanges has been the conceptualisation of the online platform as a 'virtual third space'. The 'third space' is another idea drawn from the work of Bhabha and developed by intercultural educators such as Claire Kramsch (e.g. Kramsch & Uryu, 2020). The third space is conceived as a contact zone between cultures that offers its inhabitants a new perspective on the familiar and unfamiliar. Menard-Warwick *et al.* (2013: 966) begin their discussion of a telecollaboration project by reiterating that cultures are social constructs shaped by historical events. It is, then, from this standpoint that participants begin to interact in the third space, that is, '[...] students decenter from their linguistic and cultural world to consider their own situatedness from the perspective of another'. Through the connection of classrooms in different parts of the world, participants in telecollaborative activities co-create a virtual third space, allowing students to experience '[...] simultaneously being and not being there' (Menard-Warwick *et al.*, 2013: 967). As participants learn to inhabit and explore the liminal 'third space', they develop their intercultural competence.

## Autonomy and reflection

Garcia (2012) argues that telecollaborative activities also maximise the language teaching/learning process by giving participants space to experience and exercise autonomy and reflection. The value of telecollaborations lies in the possibility such projects bring to the enrichment of:

> classroom activities, involving linguistic and intercultural objectives, allowing learners to develop autonomous and reflective behaviors, becoming participants and responsible for their knowledge. (Garcia, 2012: 484)

Garcia's views echo those of Ware (2005), who also maintains that internet-mediated communication tools are a viable alternative to the physical classroom in that they meet a broad range of pedagogical objectives. Ware (2005: 3) states that the internet helps to enrich traditional printed materials and, more importantly, 'allows for the creation of meaningful, rich forums for interaction in which students have personal interactions'. By personalising the learning experience, online exchanges motivate learners to explore and reflect on their learning increasingly autonomously.

## Challenges and obstacles

However, despite all the attractive learning possibilities that a telecollaboration project might seem to offer, many organisers and instructors acknowledge ruefully that online exchanges are challenging to establish and implement. Simply connecting learners from different cultures via an internet platform does not guarantee learning of language or intercultural skills and attitudes. A number of tensions can interfere in the quality of the interaction and in its results. Ware (2005) identifies three aspects that can influence the effectiveness of a telecollaboration: (i) differences in the way members of each culture involved in the exchange value the teaching of foreign languages; (ii) the type of previous experience with the communication tool; and (iii) institutional differences that mark the teaching of languages at each end.

These reservations have been borne out by numerous practitioners; for example, in one project already mentioned, Alareer *et al.* (2022) chose Facebook as a means to connect university students in Brazil and

Palestine in an online exchange. The platform was chosen by the organisers owing to its global popularity as a social network site. It remained popular among most Palestinian participants. However, Brazilians' interest in Facebook has been decreasing over the past years as they migrate to other social media apps, and this difference in attitude towards the value of the platform was reported by some participants as contributing, in part, to their gradual disengagement from the Brazil–Palestine project.

In addition to factors such as the choice of platform and differing attitudes to language learning, another aspect that can change the results of the interaction is the period of time dedicated to the planning and implementation of the online exchanges. The pedagogical literature on online exchanges shows that there are telecollaboration projects of quite different durations, ranging from, say, three weeks to three entire academic years. There is little or no hard evidence on how long an online exchange should last before it bears fruit in terms of enhanced linguistic or intercultural competence. It is clear from experience of such exchanges, however, that it takes time to build rapport between participants of an intercultural project. So, if teachers want their groups to engage in more complex topics and put their skills of discovery, negotiation and interpretation into practice, they should be ready to keep their project going for a substantial period of time. Ware (2005: 4) suggests, 'successful online communication requires that students sustain their engagement in intercultural interaction across at least several weeks or longer'. Lima and Dart (2019) describe successful online exchanges that run between six and 10 weeks.

Despite the obvious attractions of telecollaborations in affording virtual 'third spaces' for the development of intercultural communicative competence, autonomy and reflection, most organisers and instructors experience frustrations in establishing and implementing them. This book is intended to alert readers to some of the more common challenges and obstacles, and give some advice on how to overcome them. There will always be challenges, obstacles and frustrations; however, there are also ways of coping with them, and even, at times, turning them to advantage.

## Interculturality and the Role of Education

Finally, it is worth reflecting briefly on the forces that have positioned interculturality at the heart of the language teaching agenda. Two simultaneous but distinct phenomena have marked the way that diverse social and cultural groups have built and maintained their relationships in recent decades: physical migration and the spread of communication devices connected to the internet, particularly the smartphone. Unlike other eras, when migration to another country almost always implied, for migrants, a complete rupture with the originary culture, it is now possible, through different communication technologies, for migrants to maintain a strong connection with their geographically distant home community.

Indeed, it is possible to argue that the experience of keeping a computer-mediated connection among communities across geographical space impacts on both the home culture and the host culture, since it allows people to engage in 'transnational networks that offer potentially altered forms of identity, community formation and cooperation' (Blommaert & Rampton, 2012: 9). Similarly, Geertz (1986) observes that issues inherent to cultural diversity, which previously emerged from the interaction *between* societies, are now increasingly situated *within* them. This is so because, according to Geertz:

> social and cultural boundaries coincide less and less closely – there are Japanese in Brazil, Turks on the Main, and West Indian meets East in the streets of Birmingham – a shuffling process which has of course been going on for quite some time (Belgium, Canada, Lebanon, South Africa – and the Caesarsí Rome was not all that homogeneous), but which is, by now, approaching extreme and near universal proportions. (Geertz, 1986: 265)

The fact that, increasingly, mixed communities share geographical space and routinely communicate instantaneously across it means that it is no longer enough to just acknowledge the existence of diversity in our societies. Since intercultural interaction is inevitable, it makes sense to address it as a rich learning opportunity, with the aim of helping the individual to understand effectively how social, cultural and political relations are currently arranged, in order to establish a better dialogue between people of different backgrounds, beliefs and values. An urgent contemporary pedagogical agenda is to confront ethnocentric points of view, which work on the assumption that identities are static and pre-determined, and which may lead to extremist positions that consider cultural difference as a justification for marginalisation, exclusion, oppression and violence. Educators have a responsibility not just to teach 'tolerance' but to seek opportunities for learners to engage with otherness, with a view to establishing empathy and solidarity. Towards this end, as we have argued in this chapter, online intercultural exchanges build on the familiar affordances of computer-mediated communication to bring members of disparate communities together in dialogue.

## Conclusion

This chapter has offered a framework for what follows by introducing online intercultural exchanges and explaining their role in promoting the development of linguistic and intercultural competence. We have acknowledged that telecollaborations can vary in definition, format, task types and duration, and they can use different platforms. The range of online intercultural exchanges currently practised exceeds those illustrated in this handbook. Even so, the advice given in this volume assumes some common normative practices. We assume that organisers and instructors will want to build an online exchange to develop both linguistic and intercultural competences. Chapters 2 and 3 discuss the initial process of finding willing partners and agreeing the goals of the exchange with them. We assume that they will choose one single platform for their exchange, the topic of Chapter 4. Issues of conduct, ethics and security are covered in Chapter 5.

Whatever the platform chosen, most online exchanges opt for asynchronous interactions through written texts, or 'posts'. Asynchronous writing is a popular choice for online intercultural exchanges not only 'because it allows teachers to cope with constraints such as time differences, but also because, in less proficient classes, it gives students the chance to review, rethink and rewrite their texts' (Lima & Dart, 2019: 168). Most of the activities in this volume, then, assume that participants will communicate asynchronously via written texts, no doubt augmented by visuals such as emojis, gifs, photos and video clips. Chapters 6–10 address topics relevant to the actual implementation of an online intercultural exchange: breaking the ice among participants, designing intercultural tasks, encouraging rapport, understanding the role of the instructor and dealing with problems that might arise.

The biggest disadvantage of asynchronous collaborations is that they are not as dynamic as many groups wish them to be. Especially when younger participants are involved in the initiative, motivation tends to fade after a few weeks of exchange. Organisers might therefore consider arranging at least one synchronous meeting in the course of a telecollaboration. Chapter 11 gives advice on the issues to consider when setting up a synchronous video link as part of a longer, largely asynchronous exchange.

Finally, Chapters 12–14 address topics that extend beyond the duration of the exchange itself. Chapter 12 considers how the data elicited from participants during an online exchange can feed into subsequent language awareness activities. Chapter 13 considers how participants' performance might be assessed, and Chapter 14 provides some guidance on evaluating the success or otherwise of an exchange. Finally, as some readers will wish to use their experience of online intercultural exchanges for further study or publication, Chapter 15 offers some general advice on action research and telecollaborations, particularly aimed at readers who are interested in pursuing graduate studies in this area.

# 2 Finding Partners

Embarking on a telecollaborative project presents several immediate challenges to organisers and instructors. They need to decide, for example, which platform to use, whether the format of the exchange will be synchronous or asynchronous and whether or not there will be video meetings among participants. But the first issue to be addressed is simply finding suitable and willing partners for the telecollaboration. This chapter focuses on the considerable challenge of identifying such partners, with regard not only to the initial arrangements for running the online exchange, but also maintaining the groups' engagement with the common objective of an intercultural communication mediated by the internet.

In this chapter, we look at some case studies that illustrate situations that can facilitate or compromise a telecollaborative partnership, be it in the beginning or during the implementation of a project. For this, we draw on some actual experiences of educators who have been involved in establishing online exchanges. The aim of this chapter is to indicate to readers some of the issues they are likely to face, and possible ways of building successful connections.

## Exploiting Personal Connections

To be frank, in our experience, the qualities most useful to novices who are about to embark on organising an online exchange are perseverance, resilience and luck. Many of us have been drawn into developing online intercultural exchanges through enthusiasm and idealism. Interaction with our peers in negotiating a partnership often results in a dampening down of our initial enthusiasm and compromises that dilute our idealism. In some cases, the lack of alignment between partners leads to unfulfilled expectations, disappointment, loss of interest and eventual discontinuance of the partnership. However, with resilience, perseverance and an open mind, partnerships can develop in a fruitful and satisfying way. The early discussions with potential partners are often the most complex and they set the tone for what follows.

We have found that the strongest and most enduring partnerships tend to develop among educators who are already part of the same social or professional network, that is, they are already associated in some way, personally or professionally. Individuals can actively become part of useful networks by joining professional associations or organisations of teachers, reaching out to research centres and groups, taking part in international workshops for teachers or finding out about collaboration agreements signed between their own and other educational institutions. One example of the fortunate happenstance that results in a strong partnership is recounted in Dart (2015): his first idea for a telecollaboration arose when he travelled from Brazil to England to participate in a professional development course. There, he befriended a Polish colleague who was also interested in the idea, and, once they returned to their home countries, an online intercultural exchange between Rio and Warsaw was born. The strength of the online connection is bound up in the initial personal connection that ensured their goals and expectations for the project were similar, and that they could openly discuss potential issues as they arose.

Our observations and experience also lead us to the conclusion that effective collaborative networks increase in a spiral-like way: enthusiastic individuals and groups involved in a successful exchange might continue to meet others at conferences or seminars, and they act as contacts, bridges and intermediaries for newcomers who wish to join a project, or they act as catalysts in the merging of projects. Lima and Dart (2019) recount the process whereby two smaller online exchanges (including the Warsaw–Rio connection) came together in a larger project, in part because they were introduced to each other personally at a teachers' conference by a mutual acquaintance who knew they were engaged in similar activities.

## Using an Agency

Without personal or professional contacts, those who are seeking partners do require luck and tenacity. One strategy is to turn to one of various websites and online agencies that offer to link up organisers and instructors. By 'agency' we simply mean groups that have been set up to promote online exchanges and help find partners; some of these are suggested in Figure 2.1. These agencies are suitable for various groups of participants of different ages and at different levels of education. Some have particular themes, e.g. 'iearn' invites collaborations that address the United Nations Educational, Scientific and Cultural Organisation's (UNESCO) Sustainable Development Goals.

While such agencies may well be a successful means of finding telecollaboration partners for many educators, not all attempts to use them bear fruit. One of the authors of this handbook (Lima), in the past, did attempt to find partners through a website created specifically for

The following websites currently offer to find partners for telecollaboration:

- Asia Pacific Virtual Exchange Association: https://apvea.org/
- Collaborative Online International Learning: https://coil.suny.edu/
- Cultura: http://cultura.mit.edu/
- epals: https://www.epals.com/
- iearn: https://iearn.org/
- LinguaeLive: http://www.linguaelive.ca/
- The Mixxer: https://www.language-exchanges.org/
- Soliya: https://soliya.net/
- Stevens Initiative: http://www.stevensinitiative.org/
- Teleplaza: https://teleplaza.commons.gc.cuny.edu/
- Teletandem Brasil: http://www.teletandembrasil.org/
- UniCollaborate: https://www.unicollaboration.org/index.php/finding-a-ve-partner/
- The Virtual Exchange Coalition: http://virtualexchangecoalition.org/

**Figure 2.1** Agencies that help find telecollaboration partners

language teachers interested in telecollaboration. It looked promising: on the site, the user, usually a teacher, could create a profile and give information about their proposed telecollaboration project (e.g. the age group and class of the students involved, the discipline and/or subjects they intended to address and the language[s] through which participants would interact). The user also had to provide a brief description of the project before making it available on the website. Following these steps, the user could register the proposed project, making it visible to potential partners around the world.

Until 2014, the agency concerned provided all participants with secure email accounts to prevent use of their personal addresses. At the time of writing, interactions now take place through posts in discussion forums moderated by the instructors who collaborate on the project. All instructors who collaborate must submit a profile for analysis by the platform moderators before being approved, to protect the safety of the participants.

Such agencies are clearly professional in their organisation and, when effective, they have the potential to link partners who were hitherto unknown to each other, by making available suitable project descriptions and providing a platform for interaction. However, there is no guarantee that potential partners will come forward, and engagement by the partners is, of course, voluntary. In Lima's case, after two months, no potential partner responded to the project summary he had posted, and there was no response to his attempts to reach out to those who had proposed other projects. This particular attempt to create a telecollaboration via the agency was therefore, reluctantly, abandoned. This is not to say that this and similar agencies could not be used to develop successful partnerships; simply, that the organiser or instructor who seeks to use such an agency or website should be prepared for possible disappointment and so might also need to consider alternative strategies.

## Using Institutional Contacts

Another approach to finding partners is to explore and exploit institutional contacts of various kinds. Again, Lima turned at one time to colleagues and former undergraduates who had spent time abroad, to identify possible telecollaborators for a group in Brazil. Through institutional contacts, he reached out to a high school teacher, based in the eastern United States, who had once been part of an exchange programme in Brazil. This seemed, at first, like an ideal partnership, though neither, at the time, had any experience of telecollaboration.

Despite, or perhaps because of, their mutual lack of experience, expectations for the telecollaborative project ran high. They agreed to use a simple email platform as the means of communication between participants, and they decided to fully integrate their online exchange into classroom activities and promote 'real' contact between representatives of different languages and cultures. In so doing, they sought to enact some of the fundamental principles of telecollaboration that they had read about in papers such as O'Dowd (2003), Belz and Thorne (2006) and Garcia (2012).

The initial correspondence between Lima and the potential American co-organiser, then, suggested a promising outlook for the project. However, as Lima began to spell out in detail how he envisaged the collaboration would proceed, and as it became clear how frequent the contact would need to be in order to implement an effective exchange, the prospective American partner's enthusiasm cooled. Her messages grew scarcer until they stopped completely. No clear reason was given for the loss of interest. It may be that Lima had inadvertently displayed his political values or ideological attitudes that undermined the respect and empathy required for an effective partnership (cf. Corbett, 2010: 7), or it might simply have been that the institutional differences became more apparent and were construed as an obstacle to partnership (cf. Ware, 2005). Whatever the reason, it is clear that would-be organisers and instructors also need to deploy their own intercultural skills in seeking promising partners for telecollaboration. Again, we offer this cautionary tale to stress that telecollaborations often grow more easily among members of established social and professional networks, rather than among relative strangers. It is not impossible for strangers to become co-organisers, but the work involved in developing trust (see below) is often harder.

## Partnering with an Experienced Telecollaborator

Luck often accompanies tenacity. Happily, Lima persevered in his search for a suitable institutional contact, finally establishing an effective partnership after reading an article by another American professor about her experience with telecollaboration; the article also contained her email address. After emailing her, Lima managed, at last, to set up a productive telecollaboration between his high school pupils and university students in an English for global communication course in the United States. In some respects, this looked as if it would be an unpromising partnership; Ware (2005) suggests that one obstacle to effective telecollaboration is institutional difference (e.g. between higher and secondary educational levels). However, the expertise of the American partner was a positive factor in addressing and surmounting potential obstacles and the resulting exchange was a success.

## Developing Trust

One thing to take into account in developing exchanges, particularly among relatively inexperienced partners who have no previous personal or professional acquaintance, is the time required to align expectations and goals. In the case of the successful partnership between the Brazilian and American organisers, no fewer than 32 emails were exchanged after Lima's initial contact, during which the potential partners exchanged information about themselves and their teaching contexts, and began to plan their activities in detail. The emails were eventually followed by a Skype meeting, in which the two organisers continued to discuss the nature of the collaboration face to face. During the Skype meeting, the American partner informed Lima that she would have three assistants working with her, and they also discussed their roles.

These case studies of failure and success are presented as concrete illustrations of general precepts that have been expressed by educators such as Müller-Hartmann (2000) and O'Dowd (2003), namely, that organisers and instructor need to take time to build trust and to ensure that they stay in tune during the planning stages. Garcia (2012: 483) clearly expresses the attitude of cooperation required by online exchanges when he states that 'working collaboratively implies committing to the task of learning and, at the same time, committing to the other in a mutual and reciprocal manner'. The time taken to demonstrate this commitment needs to be budgeted for. Trust arises through an investment of time and energy in clarifying goals and expectations (see further, Chapter 4).

## Conclusion

We have drawn on our own personal experiences of different ways of finding telecollaboration partners to illustrate what can go right and wrong in the process. It is possible to seek partners through various agencies, through institutional contacts and by 'cold calling' those who have expertise in the area, but the most dependable route in our experience is by taking advantage of personal and professional contacts in one's own networks. None is guaranteed to work, and each takes effort to sustain. Futhermore, finding willing partners is only the first step in the process of developing an effective online exchange. The next steps involve choosing a suitable online platform, aligning goals and expectations, ensuring the safety of the participants and developing tasks for them to undertake. These are the topics of the following chapters.

# 3 Choosing an Appropriate Platform

One of the earliest and most important decisions to be made when setting up a telecollaboration is the choice of platform. There are many possible platforms for an online intercultural exchange, ranging from simple email to social media to bespoke telecollaboration platforms such as Google Classroom and Canvas. Selecting an appropriate one will have a major impact on how engaged the participants will be with the exchange, which in turn will affect the frequency and quality of their contributions. This chapter offers some practical advice about the choice of platform, again based largely on the experience of the authors of this handbook. After experimenting with a number of alternatives with different groups, over the decades, we have identified some of the main advantages and disadvantages associated with different platforms. This chapter synthesises what we have learned and suggests some basic criteria that should help organisers and instructors to choose an appropriate platform for their own telecollaborations.

## Basic Criteria

The first thing to note is that, from simple email to social media, from videoconferencing applications (apps) to learning management systems (LMSs), such as Moodle, no one platform is absolutely ideal, and no platform that is currently widely available has been specifically designed to facilitate online intercultural exchanges as such. Rather, possible platforms were designed for other purposes, e.g. to allow fast digital communication, develop social networks of friends and colleagues or facilitate online learning in general. It is true that some – such as Moodle, Blackboard, Google Classroom and Canvas – are primarily educational in intent, but they are not primarily designed to enable telecollaboration among participants from different cultures. Therefore, while a number of factors need to be taken into account (e.g. do you have institutional access to an LMS, and can access also be allowed for those outside your institution?), as you assess the advantages and disadvantages of each option, having a clear view of the specific aims of your telecollaboration project, and of who your participants are, will help you to make the best practical choice.

Two overarching criteria to consider are convenience and accessibility. Participants' sense of engagement will be affected by their familiarity with the platform and whether they like it or whether they need to install a new app on their devices and learn how to use it. We hardly need to observe that technological tools such as apps and their popularity change constantly and quickly. A platform that is seemingly ubiquitous today may very well be obsolete in a few years, if not months. In our own case, not so long ago, we were all ready to begin a new exchange using a long-established platform called Edmodo, only to receive an email notifying us that it would shortly be discontinued. Particular age groups, perhaps especially teenagers, can also be highly sensitive to trends. One simple way of choosing a platform is to ask prospective participants what kind of digital communications or app they are mainly using today, and to consider whether that can be adapted for use in a telecollaboration.

With that proviso, having tried out over the years most of the main types of platform that organisers and instructors might use for telecollaboration, we summarise the pros and cons of each. Although much of the following will be familiar to readers, and most of it is common sense, it is worth reviewing what we know when choosing a suitable platform for telecollaboration.

## Email and Direct Messaging Platforms

Dating from the early 1970s, and so one of the oldest surviving forms of online communication, email remains an essential work instrument, particularly for many older professionals, but it is fair to say that it is not now the preferred means of communication among younger generations. Social media applications such as WhatsApp and WeChat, on the other hand, remain extremely popular at the time of writing. Although it might seem odd to group together those two forms of communication, they actually have a lot in common, insofar as their essential purpose is to allow direct contact, individually or in groups, with the possibility of attaching image, audio and video files.

A clear advantage of email or instant messaging apps is that, in some form, they are almost universally accessible and they remain a basic online tool. Even those who are too young to have email as part of their preferred communicative repertoire will have had to use an account in order to register for a variety of online services. Thus, though no longer popular as a medium, email remains one possible platform for online exchanges, when other platforms are, for whatever reason, unavailable.

One of the earliest guides to telecollaboration, Warschauer (1995) includes some descriptions of ways in which email was used for online exchanges in the earlier years of their emergence as a means of learning language and culture. A number of telecollaborations simply involve participants interacting with 'keypals' on an individual basis and using that relationship as a means to explore each other's life, language and culture. The individual basis of this kind of exchange facilitates 'tandem' learning whereby two participants communicate in the other's language in order to improve each other's linguistic competences. For example, among Warschauer's collection of activities, Jennifer Ham (1995) describes a 'composition and conversation' activity using email that connected learners of advanced German in an American university with German undergraduates who were taking classes in American studies. She explains the procedure as follows:

> After learning appropriate vocabulary, reading short literary passages and surveys on the subject, and discussing the topic [of how Americans and Germans perceived each other] extensively amongst themselves and with their instructor, students were put into pairs and asked to formulate particular aspects of the topic they felt they either would like more varied input on or further reaction to. Each group of two students was given two e-mail addresses, one from a native German speaker studying American Studies at our German exchange university in Kassel and the other from one of our own students enrolled in a study-abroad experience at the same university. The pair of students was given the task of creating a mini-discussion group including themselves and their new overseas partners. Communicating in German via e-mail, the students were to introduce themselves, explain the project of field study, and facilitate discussion by eliciting reactions on the subject from the group for one week. They then sent copies of the responses they received from Germany to other students in the class. Out of this pool of letters shared by the whole class, students selected interesting excerpts and summarized their findings in a short writing assignment. (Ham, 1995: 107)

While the technology involved in this project might appear antiquated to readers today, and its use perhaps cumbersome, the procedures could well be adapted to other platforms, particularly instant messaging apps. Participants in the exchange can be grouped and given joint tasks to perform, the outcomes being shared with their own or another class.

Even so, email and instant messaging are probably unlikely to be the preferred platform for online exchanges. As we have said, while email is relatively universally available, it is generally used for work purposes by older users and not by the younger generations. While teenagers, in particular, may resist using an old-fashioned medium such as email, or simply forget to access it on a regular basis, older participants might lose track of the messages related to the exchange amid the many they are likely to receive daily for work purposes. One additional problem with using an email group for an exchange is that a string of email messages may not be particularly conducive to prolonged engagement. After a few email exchanges, it could well become hard to keep track of the conversation, which leads to demotivation. As we write, messaging apps are currently the preferred mode of communication; however, some messaging apps are presently partially restricted to particular regions of the world (e.g. WhatsApp in the West, WeChat in China). Public preferences are inevitably subject to fashion and change as innovative apps become available and vie for users. The choice of platform then requires negotiation and compromise. In our experience, many potential participants, even younger ones, are unwilling to download a new messaging app purely to engage in an online intercultural exchange. If the exchange requires participants to do so, then their motivation to participate might be limited.

It must be said that none of the problems outlined here means that instant messaging apps or email cannot be appropriate platforms for an intercultural exchange. They do suggest that their best chance of working well is with smaller groups of more mature and more motivated participants, whose members are already comfortable with the technology being used. As is also the case with the other options we examine below, the characteristics of the group will largely determine the choice of platform.

## Social Media Apps

The current popularity of social networking websites and apps among potential participants in intercultural exchanges, especially younger participants, is both their greatest advantage and their biggest drawback. From the advent of Facebook in 2004, social media use has become one of the most popular ways of spending leisure time around the globe. Currently, popular social media sites include Instagram, TikTok (Douyin in China), Twitter (or 'X'), Vimeo and YouTube. In China, currently, Bilibili has overtaken Youku as the preferred platform for video sharing, while Xiaohongshu ('Little Red Book') is described on its own website as a 'user-generated content community focusing on shopping experiences'.

Social media apps allow individuals to group together to share content that they download or generate. One possible procedure to follow in order to hold an exchange on a social media platform is to create a dedicated group or page within the social networking site. After participants are added or invited to join, tasks are then posted at regular intervals (see Figure 3.1 for an example from Facebook). It is extremely important to ensure that the organisers or instructors manage the pages, and that they choose the correct settings for the group. Attention to such details is necessary to guarantee the safety of participants, as we discuss further in Chapter 5, especially if children or younger teenagers are involved.

Here is my bedroom also my studying area too. I always work homework and read books for 2 hours everyday. I love reading novel especially the Sherlock Holmes because he is the greatest detective in the world.

It's great that you save some time every day to read. I love the Sherlock Holmes stories! Have you managed to figure out a mystery before he does? 😄 (Don't think that's possible...but maybe?)

**Figure 3.1**  A post and response from a Facebook exchange

The familiarity of participants with social media platforms and the degree to which they enjoy using them can be significant in motivating them, making contributing to the online exchange appear to be intrinsically attractive and fun. However, the very fact that learners are already in the habit of accessing the website or app for several other reasons during the day also increases the chance that they will become distracted and forget to check the messages from the exchange group on a regular basis. On the other hand, many users will often go online to check their social media and this frequency of access might also regularly bring them back to the exchange.

One issue regarding social networks is how fleeting their popularity can be. Since we started carrying out intercultural exchanges, we have seen the rise and fall of apps on which many of our students, at some point, seemed to spend most of their waking hours. These were then abandoned in favour of other, newer ones, whose own success, in turn, is clearly not going to last forever. Thus, many participants who once might have been absorbed in Facebook now see it as a place for their parents' generation and join all their friends daily on Instagram or TikTok. Such changes in fashion are unlikely to be a problem within a single edition of an online exchange, but they should be taken into consideration for longer-term planning: organisers should be aware that an app that recently motivated and excited participants might not have the same impact on a new cohort of users. The differences that exist among social networks make them more or less appropriate for the kinds of activities in which organisers will want their learners to engage.

Social media websites and apps are designed to facilitate immediate interaction and certain forms of sharing content, but they can be unsuited – or they might simply be perceived by participants to be inappropriate – for more 'academic' tasks. Even so, the application of some creative thinking can be enough to bring about ways to adapt tasks to the chosen platform. For example, collaborative tasks in which participants are asked to post additional content at regular intervals and then increasingly build on what has been added might become engaging and dynamic if proper preparation is made and guidance is given.

A final but substantial issue regarding social media is their ethical and political associations. As we write, the availability of the popular TikTok app is being restricted in the West for political reasons. While social messaging apps allow information and communication to flow freely among users, legitimate issues around privacy, personal security and the exploitation of user data concern some potential users, or some of the parents of potential users. Some parents might wish to restrict younger users' access to certain social media. At the very least, users should be made aware of 'netiquette' and the appropriate use of social media (see further, Chapter 5). Moreover, the ubiquity of some social networks in one region can sometimes give the misleading impression that they are available everywhere. At the time of writing, Facebook and YouTube are not available in China, nor are those social media that are ubiquitous in China (e.g. WeChat Moments) necessarily used elsewhere. Organisers need to communicate with their partners to find out if their preferred platform is popular – or even available – in another region of the globe if they wish to interact with participants from that region.

## Learning Management Systems

Unlike email and social media, some platforms are specifically created for educational purposes. LMSs such as Canvas, Moodle and Google Classroom saw their number of users grow significantly as a direct consequence of the massive shift to online teaching that took place during and after 2020 because of the COVID-19 pandemic. As a consequence, many organisers are now more familiar with these educational platforms and their affordances than they might otherwise have been. Figure 3.2 shows

Hi again, guys!

I chose to share with you a well-known recipe here in Brazil: Goiabada or Doce de Goiaba (Guava or Guava Jam). This candy is made with just 3 ingredients: Guavas, water and sugar. All you need to do is beat the Guavas with sugar and water (but just a little bit), so it won't be too difficult to stir the candy. Then the mixture goes to medium heat for a while and then it must be cooled for 12 hours. In the end, it will look like this:

Here in Brazil, many people (including myself) have the habit of eating candies (usually cold desserts) after lunch which is a hot meal. In my region, some people (especially the elderly), even drink cold water after eating the candy after lunch.

See ya! ;)

**Figure 3.2**   Post from Canvas, a virtual learning management system

a screenshot from a Canvas discussion of favourite dishes from around the world.

For example, one important advantage of LMSs over the other options we have been describing is the fact that they have been designed specifically to enable interaction between learners and instructors. When participants log into the platform, they find an online environment which, by design, creates a classroom-like experience. With no distractions and no uses for the website other than its primary function, the time spent on an LMS is likely to be entirely dedicated to educational assignments, in this case, intercultural activities. Participants are more likely to take the activities seriously if the site is not directly associated with leisure or entertainment. On the other hand, users are less likely to 'drop into' an LMS in the way that they regularly drop into their preferred social media sites.

Unlike social media, LMSs are primarily meant for two-way communication between instructors and their pupils, although group work features can be enabled under certain conditions. Compared with social media, LMS organisers can more easily set up assessments and quizzes and keep track of participants. The LMS format is suitable for various sorts of educational activities, but this itself can make it more challenging for the coordinators of an intercultural exchange project to foster the continuous interaction among participants that is of paramount importance for success.

Some LMSs are more likely to be provided by institutions and are not otherwise available for personal use – Blackboard and Moodle tend to fall into this category. Institutional permission would normally be required for 'outsiders' to be registered onto an online exchange. Individual organisers and instructors, however, can register online to use other LMSs, such as Google Classroom and Canvas. Geographical restrictions can again come into play; at present, Google Classroom is not available in China, whereas Canvas is. There are drawbacks to using commercial providers of LMSs in that their availability can be unpredictable. In order to work with Chinese partners, the authors of this volume switched from Google Classrooms to Edmodo. After a successful couple of years, the platform abruptly announced that it was 'sunsetting', or closing, which required a quick shift to an alternative platform (in our case, Canvas) just before an exchange was scheduled to begin. A degree of flexibility is always necessary to overcome unpredictable issues.

## Videoconferencing Apps

Email, social media apps and LMSs are all largely used for asynchronous interaction among exchange participants. For real-time encounters, Skype, Zoom and TenCent Meeting (or Voov) are currently popular platforms for videoconferencing, and all have much to offer online intercultural exchanges. Videoconferencing apps now allow interaction in a variety of modes: lecture based, group discussions, breakout rooms, chats and giving responses such as applauding, liking, etc. Videoconferencing has unique advantages over all the other platforms surveyed in this chapter in that it is currently as close as telecollaboration can possibly get to meeting people, either in our home town or theirs (although virtual reality [VR] is quickly developing as an immersive form of potential telecollaboration). Videoconferencing is, in a way, 'face-to-face' interaction, with abundant opportunities for users to explore each other's environment to the extent they are willing to allow access. Paradoxically, however, that very same feature is one of several possible downsides of videoconferencing.

First of all, bringing strangers 'inside' our homes is not always something with which people are comfortable. From the concern over what is visible in the background to potentially embarrassing appearances by relatives or pets, the degree to which we feel we are exposing ourselves to the scrutiny of others can be a source of discomfort. While participants in online exchanges might indeed be excited about sharing their working, school or domestic surroundings with their partners, we must not assume that this will always be the case. Instructors need to be sensitive to possible concerns among participants about revealing more about their working and living conditions than they feel comfortable with.

Furthermore, two kinds of technical limitations can constrain videoconferences, the first being the need for all participants to be available at the same time. It is likely that instructors will be dealing with learners from different time zones, and arranging for everyone to be online simultaneously can be challenging or unfeasible. People might be willing to adapt their schedules and access the platform at a time of day which is unusual for them, but that will not necessarily be a practical solution on a regular basis.

Another possible challenge is access to the necessary hardware – namely, cameras and microphones – and bandwidth, as well as internet speed. Most readers of this book will be well aware that online interactions can easily be limited or compromised by poor connections or a malfunctioning microphone or camera. Such circumstances make it difficult to depend on videoconferencing for the exchange to occur, and may result in a frustrating rather than a satisfying experience.

That said, face-to-face meetings among participants in an online intercultural exchange, even if they are only occasional, can be highly motivating and enjoyable – and the possibilities are discussed further in Chapter 11. However, at the present time, it is not likely that many sustained online intercultural exchanges will be held entirely by videoconference.

## Conclusion

Based on the above sections, we offer a brief checklist for organisers and instructors who are engaged in choosing a current platform for use with participants. Once partners have been found, these are the among the pressing issues to discuss.

- Accessibility: Can participants in all the exchange locations access the platform?
- Ease of use: Can participants easily learn how to use the platform? Will they be familiar with it already?
- Popularity: Will participants actively want to access the platform? Do they do so already?
- Appropriate seriousness: Is the platform associated with interactions at the level of seriousness that instructors and participants expect of the exchange?
- Functionality: Does the platform allow participants and instructors to do the kinds of things they want to do, e.g. post text, images and videos; make quizzes; conduct surveys?
- Security: Does the platform enable users to maintain an appropriate level of privacy, security and comfort?
- Innovation: Is the platform seen as dated, its technology outmoded or is it regarded as innovative and exciting?
- Immediacy: Depending on whether the exchange (or part of it) is synchronous or asynchronous, does the platform allow instant messaging, or even live streaming?

As communications technologies continue to develop, the affordances of different platforms will change. Some educational institutions are already experimenting with VR headsets – some of which can be obtained at a reasonable cost and used in conjunction with learners' smartphones. Participants in some online exchanges are offering their partners an immersive virtual experience of their everyday lives (Melchor-Couto & Herrera, 2023). Ultimately, then, the organisers of online intercultural exchanges need to keep the lines of communication open among themselves, with their changing waves of participants and learners, and with those who are experimenting with new platforms elsewhere. The choice of platform will evolve over time and be a result of a series of ongoing conversations.

# 4 Agreeing Goals

At the same time as new partners in a telecollaboration are agreeing on a suitable platform, they will also be discussing the goals they wish to achieve through the online intercultural exchange. For some partners, these goals may be fully integrated with a broader language and culture curriculum that is being followed by the learners, or they might be separate from and supplementary to the curriculum followed in class. Partners may be subject to different institutional demands in this respect. For an online intercultural exchange to work, it is important that organisers and instructors – and participants – share a common sense of the purpose of the exchange. This chapter considers the process of agreeing goals by reviewing some of the possible outcomes that an online intercultural exchange might be expected to achieve. These – or similar goals – can become the basis of initial discussions among organisers and instructors.

## Aligning Objectives

As is the case with any sort of collaboration, an essential stage in the initial process is making sure that all parties involved in the intercultural exchange agree on its learning objectives. For the novice organiser or instructor who decides to initiate or join such a project, the possibility of promoting contact among learners from different places may at first seem to be its own reward, but there ought to be more specific, achievable objectives that educators and participants aim to reach. Participants, in particular, should have a concrete sense that they are enriching their linguistic and cultural knowledge through the interactions. Otherwise, once the immediate novelty of the exchange wears off, participants may start losing interest and their contributions will drop in frequency and quality.

The aims that will be negotiated among the organisers and instructors, and, at a different stage, with the participants are, naturally, dependent on the circumstances of all those who are to be involved in the initiative. Their age, language proficiency level, familiarity with the digital platform and capacity to access it regularly are some of the factors which will impact on the kinds of outcome that can be expected. The duration of the intercultural exchange is also a factor in determining what can realistically be achieved.

As at least two distinct groups of people will be directly involved in the exchange, at least two sets of objectives need to be established and aligned. The first set of objectives is what the organisers and instructors hope to accomplish. Few steps are as easy or as dangerous to overlook as going over those goals in the initial stages, for organisers may simply assume that their counterparts see the intercultural exchange in the same way as they do. When that turns out not to be the case, misunderstandings may lead to disappointment, reproaches and clashes which might, in turn, jeopardise the implementation of the exchange and undermine future collaborations.

It is worth recalling at the outset that an online intercultural exchange can be set up to address any number of pedagogical objectives, and there is a strong possibility that it will include diverse groups of learners. Organisers will bring with them overt and implicit educational agendas that might not always be compatible. The success of the project will therefore depend on taking time to discuss with fellow organisers the explicit goals that instructors will share, and how those goals relate to the educational context of each group of participants involved. The probability of success is influenced by the thoroughness of the initial discussion about what the project is supposed to be, and by the degree of attention paid to the specific contexts of the participants.

The second set of objectives concerns what participants themselves will attempt to achieve as they engage in their interaction with those from other cultural backgrounds. Typically enthusiastic when they first join the initiative, participants benefit from having a clear idea of what to aim for as the weeks and months go by. Their goals can be as varied as their educational contexts, and are necessarily informed by them. They might consider how they will benefit from an academic standpoint, and they might also be sensitive to the ways in which their peers, friends and parents might react to their involvement. Another important factor here is to ensure that participants have a say in the shaping of goals as the exchange continues. Just as it can be motivating in traditional classrooms to involve learners in the negotiation of syllabuses (cf. Breen & Littlejohn, 2000), so participant involvement in the development of an online exchange can help maintain their active interest in it. As organisers and instructors become more experienced in running online intercultural exchanges, they also develop a keener sense of the kinds of goals that their partners and participants might wish to achieve through them.

The remaining sections of this chapter review some of the common objectives that online intercultural exchanges might seek to achieve. It is not a comprehensive or restrictive list; however, it is intended to act as a prompt for readers to reflect on what outcomes they would like to see from their own telecollaborations. Later in the chapter, we consider possible ways in which organisers and instructors can discuss the aims of the project among themselves and with the participants in the exchange. While some of the goals may relate more obviously to intercultural competences and others to language development, in practice both sets of goals are intimately connected: ultimately the goal of the exchange is for participants to engage in experiences that will help them to develop the linguistic resources necessary to interact with members of other communities, so that they can explore and investigate diverse cultures, and thus transform the way they look at the world. There are, however, numerous ways of achieving those goals.

## Institutional Goals

Any organiser or instructor of an online intercultural exchange is likely to be influenced to some extent by institutional context: most learners will follow curricula established by the institution or even by national or supranational guidelines. Even when telecollaboration organisers are high-level managers or the owners of a school, they are committed to observing the goals that they share with other stakeholders, from learners' parents to the school staff. At college or university level, online exchanges might be conducted as part of a course, or as an extracurricular activity that nevertheless will be aligned with the prevailing educational ethos, which itself might be influenced by broad curricular guidelines such as the *Common European Framework of Reference for Languages* (*CEFR*; Council of Europe, 2001; North *et al.*, 2018) or the National Council of State Supervisors for Languages–American Council on the Teaching of Foreign Languages (NCSSFL-ACTFL, 2017a, 2017b) 'can-do' statements. Organisers and instructors, then, can begin by reflecting on their own curricular assumptions. What do they expect and hope an online exchange will achieve for their participants? What kinds of skills and qualities do their current curricula expect learners to develop? How might an online exchange engage and enhance those skills and qualities? What unique opportunities might an online exchange present for instructors and participants?

## Intercultural Goals

One obvious way of describing the potential goal of an online intercultural exchange is to state that it should enable participants to enhance their intercultural communicative competence. However, as we observed in our discussion of intercultural communicative competence in Chapter 1, there are different and contested senses of what interculturality is. 'Mainstream' formulations of intercultural competence are codified by the *CEFR* and by the NCSSFL-ACTFL 'can-do' statements, and their pedagogical origins and development have been outlined by educators such as Byram (2021) and Corbett (2022). However, not all organisers and instructors will necessarily be familiar with these concepts of inter-cultural communicative competence, and, even if they are, their under-standing of them might vary. They may well have alternative concepts of interculturality that challenge the 'mainstream' formulations that describe intercultural communicative competence as specific types of knowledge, attitude and skill.

It is therefore worth taking time to ensure that all organisers have a common understanding of what their intercultural goals are, and how the exchange might achieve them. The aspects of intercultural com-municative competence outlined in Chapter 1 can serve as a basis for discussion. Even if differences exist among organisers, there are likely to be some areas of common ground. First of all, an online exchange is an opportunity for experiential learning: to explore cultural similarities and differences through interaction with others. Learning how to analyse and interpret other cultural practices and products through actual engage-ment with others helps realise the goal of enabling participants to deal confidently with diverse individuals in unfamiliar contexts.

A successful intercultural exchange will also give participants a series of opportunities to consider how their partners view them and their cul-ture, that is, opportunities to 'see ourselves as others see us'. Even those who have already spent time abroad as tourists might never have had the chance to engage in meaningful conversations with people from different countries. The sort of interaction learners get through an online exchange is unique in that it can promote diverse ways of looking at how those from other realities experience the world. A student from north-eastern Brazil can engage directly with a student under occupation in Palestine; a learner from a large city in the Greater Bay Area in southern China can interact directly with a fellow learner in a small town in Argentina.

Another fundamental precept in intercultural education is that gains in perspective also come from reflecting on one's own cultural condition-ing. As participants share their own intercultural encounters and see others do the same, the assumption is that they should be able to reflect on cultural relativity: how their sense of what is considered 'normal' and what is 'strange' is a function of a limited set of experiences and is, there-fore, mutable (Pohl, 2020). While such a broadening of perspective will benefit learners for the rest of their lives, more immediate effects might also be perceived in the language classroom, as participants become more open, curious and critical towards what they are taught.

These basic assumptions about interculturality can inform early and ongoing discussions about if and how the exchange is directly addressing intercultural goals: will the tasks chosen for participants really engage them in experiences that will require the development of the intercultural skills and qualities that the organisers and instructors expect?

## Fostering Creative, Critical and Compassionate Thinking

Having students participate in an intercultural exchange is a way for them to step back from their daily routines, which might enhance their ability to question the status quo and adopt a more active mindset. Because this kind of project provides opportunities for the exchange of ideas, unconstrained by regular classroom practices, it becomes more natural to consider alternative perspectives on task accomplishment in a playful manner and arrive at new insights (Pohl & Szesztay, 2015). In short, online exchanges can encourage creativity.

We also assume that regular interaction with online partners makes it easier for participants to move away from familiar, monocultural perspectives and engage in an empathetic understanding of otherness. If they have been used to spending their formal education as part of more or less homogeneous groups, participants might be intrigued at the discovery of just how similar and dissimilar other participants are to them in their tastes, worries and opinions. A possible goal of an online exchange therefore might simply be the exploration of viewpoints which are different from one's own. As Ilana Redstone (2022) points out, 'when we fail to recognize the moral legitimacy of a range of positions on controversial topics, disagreements about these issues inevitably become judgments about other people's character'. By leading participants to listen to those who come from diverse backgrounds, intercultural initiatives have the power to counteract the extreme divisiveness which can result in the dehumanising of others.

Again, if the shared goal among organisers is to foster creativity, empathy and compassion for diverse viewpoints, the tasks have to address this mutual aspiration explicitly. The organisers and instructors need to agree on tasks that will prompt participants to look at what is familiar to them from different angles. The tasks need to elicit diverse views and the experience of responding to them should foster empathy and compassion. Later chapters detail how such tasks can be devised and scaffolded, but the first step is for organisers and instructors to agree that this is the kind of pedagogical outcome they want.

## Developing More Autonomous Learners

The ideal goal of an online intercultural exchange is likely to be to set participants off on their own, autonomous pathways of cultural exploration and learning. Chapter 9 considers the role of the instructor in guiding or scaffolding the intercultural learning that participants engage in through the exchange. At the outset, organisers might discuss their expectations about the degree of input expected of instructors. The level of input might vary across the different groups involved in an intercultural exchange: some participants will benefit from regular face-to-face preparation and reflection on the telecollaboration, while others might engage with the exchanges more independently of their instructors.

Organisers and instructors need to agree on how they will inform participants that that they are in a supervised and safe learning environment. Empowering participants to explore the various topics in their own way can lead to an increased sense of agency which will be enhanced by the knowledge that they are not there to find a 'right' set of responses to any task, but to take the conversation as far as they wish. While some participants may feel more comfortable being given clear parameters for the completion of a task, flexibility is recommended in assessing participants' responses. Often, participants learn good practices from the imaginative responses of their peers.

One of the most desirable outcomes of the project might well be participants beginning to take a more active role in intercultural exploration and discovery. If encouraged, they may initiate their own cultural investigations within the parameters of the exchange, be it for their academic benefit or for the simple satisfaction of their curiosity. However, for this to happen, organisers and instructors need, again, to agree when and how learners are to be prompted and encouraged to take charge of their own learning.

## Engaging with Participants' Goals

While organisers and instructors will agree on a set of goals for the exchange, these will impact on the individual and group goals of participants in different and unpredictable ways. The reasons that participants have for joining an exchange will vary: some might be 'conscripts', brought in by an instructor, while others might be volunteers. Some might come from homogeneous backgrounds while others might be members of classrooms that are themselves quite diverse. Participants' motivations and their interest in contributing to the exchanges will, then, vary. Instructors therefore need to present the agreed goals of the course to participants in a way that engages them personally in the initiative.

Ideally, the organisers and instructors will have developed a 'curriculum with holes' (Brumfit, 1985: 12), that is, they leave spaces in their plan for the online exchange, and agree the means by which the participants in the telecollaboration can articulate their own goals and devise tasks that will achieve them. As these are likely to change during the exchange, the organisers, instructors and participants should periodically review the goals as the telecollaboration develops.

## Language Goals

In the online exchanges we have coordinated to date, the tasks largely involved participants writing posts to each other, asynchronously, in the target language, which in our case was English. Participants frequently post videos that demand listening skills, and on occasion, when videoconferences were attempted, participants presented information and engaged

in discussions and conversations in real time. The activity-oriented experience of telecollaboration can be structured in different ways but it lends
itself to process-based language acquisition, whereby the task is primary:
participants are encouraged to draw on their language resources directly
to accomplish the goals of the task. Rehearsal and reflection play their
part, but the core experience is for participants to regularly make optimal
use of their resources. As the demands of the task put pressure on learners
to extend their language resources, they will do so.

Since the ways that participants will choose to draw on their language
resources are relatively unpredictable, online exchanges are unlikely to
have a strict set of language goals. Experience will reveal to instructors
the kind of language that is generally useful in accomplishing different
kinds of task. It is evident, for example, that the language of emotion and
affect is crucial in establishing and maintaining rapport online (see Chapter 8). Otherwise, the specific topics covered in the tasks will determine
the language exponents most likely to be useful. The instructors might
predict and pre-teach useful vocabulary and grammatical exponents in
a rehearsal, monitor the performance of participants in accomplishing
the tasks and suggest ways of enhancing that performance in de-briefing
sessions.

One of the most significant pedagogical issues is how instructors
choose to deal with mistakes in spelling, vocabulary or grammar that
occur in online posts. Many will be evident in the posts we reproduce in
this book! As with other forms of process-based learning, we advocate
a consciousness-raising approach to error correction. That is, while
some useful forms may be pre-taught to participants, they may well
make mistakes in the online interactions. These errors can be noted by
instructors and categorised for future input into classroom instruction,
but error-correction should not impede participants' attempts to interact
online. Rather, a goal of online interaction should be that participants
are encouraged to marshal their linguistic resources and take risks in the
service of communication.

## Teaching and Learning about Specific Cultural Phenomena

Another set of goals to establish at the outset relate to what aspects
of 'culture' the organisers and instructors wish the exchange to address.
Culture is a vast and vaguely defined topic, and different online exchanges
will address it in different ways. Current ways of thinking about culture
view it as a dynamic set of behaviours rather than a set of products, such
as music, art, literature, food and dance – although these products are,
of course, the outcomes of behaviour. When deciding which aspects of
culture to cover in the exchange, organisers might wish to focus on the
active involvement of participants in cultural life, for example, what
music do they like to perform or listen to, what kind of food do they

**Figure 4.1** Post showing how to make a Brazilian dessert

enjoy cooking and eating on particular occasions, what kind of literature do they enjoy reading? Aspects of participants' everyday life are also cultural in the broader anthropological sense, and can be presented as opportunities for mutual exploration. Corbett (2010) is a resource book that suggests a number of practical ethnographic tasks inspired largely by his involvement in online exchanges. It invites the exploration of domestic and public spaces and asks participants to observe different kinds of interpersonal interaction, and to consider how topics such as sports, food, iconic figures, religion and politics represent different cultural attitudes and beliefs.

Our experience indicates that the excitement of sharing with others that which makes one's cultural context unique can be a powerful motivator for learning. Figure 4.1 shows a post by Brazilian participants in an online exchange in which they, without prompting, showed their partners a YouTube video they had produced about how to make a popular local dessert. This recipe was then successfully followed by the Polish participants, so that they were able to, literally, get a taste of another culture. From local delicacies to films and historical curiosities, those who have the opportunity to be in an intercultural exchange often end up engaging with the world in ways that go far beyond language.

## Conclusion

This chapter has stressed the importance of early goal-setting as a key part of the process of starting an online intercultural exchange. The goals of any exchange may vary and so they need to be explicitly understood and agreed on by everyone involved. Otherwise, the exchange can easily lead to disappointment and frustration. Not all goals need necessarily be treated by everyone with the same degree of importance, but all that are agreed on do need to be mutually compatible and accepted as valid by the whole group.

While agreed goals are necessary in structuring the exchange and ensuring smooth collaboration, they should not be treated reductively as determining the success or failure of any exchange. The results of inter-actions among people of diverse backgrounds are unpredictable and the best exchanges we have been involved with yield results – and often dem-onstrations of maturity and intercultural competence – that the organis-ers and instructors did not anticipate. For example, a participant will make an observation, or spark a discussion, that the instructors did not anticipate, and which may challenge the attitudes, beliefs and values of everyone in the learning community, necessitating fruitful negotiations of perspective. In this regard, the best exchanges are those in which organis-ers, instructors and participants set flexible goals and learn together.

# 5 Ethics, Netiquette and Security

The first five chapters in this guide focus on the preparatory steps that organisers and instructors need to take in order to design an effective online intercultural exchange. They need to reflect on the intertwined nature of language and culture, developing at least a working sense of what they understand by interculturality. They need to find partners and choose an appropriate platform. Then they need to address the linguistic and cultural goals of the proposed exchange with those partners, as well as with the participants of the exchange. A final preparatory step is equally important: attending to the ethics of online exchanges, considering explicitly the etiquette (or 'netiquette' as online etiquette has been dubbed) that will guide online interactions among instructors and participants. Care must be taken to protect the security of all involved, particularly those participants who are minors. This chapter considers ways in which organisers and instructors can attend to these issues.

## New Media, New Ethical Challenges

Online intercultural exchanges can be particularly sensitive forums for interaction in that they involve topics that explore, sometimes directly and sometimes indirectly, the attitudes, values and beliefs of participants who, initially, do not know much about each other. Participants are invited to put core aspects of their identity and beliefs at stake by making them available for interrogation and discussion. Establishing clear guidelines around ethics, netiquette and security helps organisers and instructors to prevent a number of serious problems. This is particularly necessary when participants are underage and therefore more vulnerable or sensitive to the content of discussions, but it is an essential element of this sort of activity in all cases.

The authors of this book are old enough to remember the early years of large-scale online communication and, while we remain in awe of its enabling power, we remain alert to the challenges it has posed to ethical codes of behaviour, to communicative norms and to the security of those who engage with it. As computer-mediated communication has become the 'new normal', a contested set of social rules around its use have gradually emerged. Those new rules take into account the characteristics of the many different sorts of online interactions, from the most to the least formal. When applied to situations in which cultural diversity is a major factor, they need to be exceptionally clear, and all instructors and participants need to understand them. As well as aligning the goals of the exchange in advance, organisers and instructors need to establish explicit rules that will guide all participants' contributions to the exchange, and to make these rules transparent to everyone in the learning community.

We will now examine the three kinds of guidelines, looking at what they mean in the context of our collective enterprise and at what might constitute desirable standards of behaviour.

## Promoting Ethical Conduct

While ethical conduct can be broadly defined as behaviour that society deems to be 'good' and 'moral', that seemingly straightforward definition is obviously complicated when viewed in relation to an inter-cultural exchange that involves instructors and participants who hold a diverse set of values, attitudes and beliefs. What is 'good' and 'moral' for one group of participants might well be contested by another. However, for an online exchange to work, all participants need to be aware of a shared set of rules of ethical conduct towards each other. A good starting point is an analogy of the kind of behaviour that would be considered proper in face-to-face interactions among individuals from different social and cultural backgrounds. When we meet and begin to interact with new people in social, educational or work environments, we tend to start from the premise that all parties are being honest and that they will attend to the face needs of the others, that is, they will deal with others on the basis of trust and politeness. Chapter 8 considers in detail some of the communicative resources required to express these qualities in online interactions in English, in order to develop rapport among participants.

Participants in online exchanges will be asked to act as primary sources of information about their respective cultures. Ethical guidance might request them to be as clear and comprehensive as they can about the information they provide and their own feelings about it. However, participants should be made aware that they also have the right to with-hold information that they do not wish to make public, for example details of their everyday lives that they consider too personal for general consumption.

Respect for intellectual property is another aspect of ethical conduct, and so participants should be encouraged to give details of any secondary sources or illustrative material that they are drawing on in their discussions. In the classroom, issues of intellectual property might be raised, for example regarding the uncited use of images, sounds or text created by third parties.

Participants also need to know the degree to which they 'own' their individual contributions. If the instructors and organisers, like the present authors, wish to reuse some of the participants' data in future research or publications (like this one), participants need to be notified and to consent to its use. This is usually done in the shape of a consent form or survey that participants actively acknowledge at the beginning of a telecollaboration. The use of participant data in action research is covered in Chapter 15. A possible template for requesting ethical conduct and also requesting consent to use data in research is given towards the end of this chapter.

## 'Netiquette'

The portmanteau term derived from 'internet' and 'etiquette' covers norms of politeness that extend beyond the core concerns of 'right' and 'wrong' that characterise ethical conduct. Netiquette also encompasses those aspects of politeness that participants consider appropriate or inappropriate. A common issue is, for example, whether or not it is appropriate to end a friendly post with an icon representing a kiss. The use of such an icon would be considered by some groups as signalling friendliness, and be inoffensive and unthreatening. Others, however, might regard the use of this icon as signalling an inappropriate degree of intimacy. Still others might understand that there are different norms in play in such usage, but be unsure of which set of norms they should adhere to.

Since there are no universally accepted norms governing polite behaviour, the online exchange has to generate its own norms, covering the interactions of the community. Often, depending on the groups, it is good practice for participants to have input into the community's norms; this at least raises awareness that there may be variant behaviour among different groups. Even so, some basic netiquette conventions might be made explicit and discussed with participants at the initial stages of the intercultural exchange. There can be some variance, but in our experience the following topics may require some time and explanation at the start of any telecollaboration.

- Forms of address: How will participants address each other? Will they use formal or informal modes of address? Will they use nicknames? How do participants prefer to be addressed?
- Formality of language: More generally, what register (formal or informal) is expected of participants in the exchange? The expected register will, in part, depend on the goals of the exchange and how instructors and participants view its purpose as, for example, either social or professional/academic.
- Use of humour: In more socially oriented exchanges, there might be ironic exchanges, sarcasm, teasing or joking that may cause

confusion or offence. While this is difficult to anticipate, the issues around humour might be raised in advance and coping strategies discussed if one participant contributes something that others find inappropriate.

- Inclusion and exclusion: Just as it is impolite in face-to-face conversation in groups to exclude someone, so in online interaction it is poor netiquette to ignore or neglect one or another participant. Participants can be primed to be inclusive, and to seek to engage with as wide a variety of partners as possible.
- Taboo topics: Culturally or politically, there may be topics that any exchange will consider off limits. These may include potentially rich topics for discussion, such as sexuality, politics, religion and human rights. While these may be central topics to many online exchanges, raising them may put certain groups of participants in difficulty or even danger. It would be naïve for organisers to think that even a telecollaboration that is 'closed' to outsiders will not be subject to surveillance or monitoring in some countries. Organisers and participants will need to agree which topics are not open for discussion, and – again – determine coping strategies if a participant does raise

---

**Netiquette**

We ask all participants in this exchange to confirm that they understand the following guide to 'netiquette' (acceptable behaviour in this online community). Participants who refuse to follow the guidelines may be prevented from further interactions in this community.

- Treat all participants with respect.
- Make sure that everyone is comfortable with the nature of the conversations.
- Do not request personal information of a sensitive nature.
- Friendly and open discussion is encouraged but special sensitivity should be practiced on certain topics including but not limited to religious beliefs, political opinions, gender issues, sexual orientation.
- No bad language is permitted.
- Use common sense and treat others how you would wish to be treated.

**Research and copyright**

We also ask all participants for permission to reproduce material that they post in research or educational articles and books.

- By participating in the project, I permit the teachers of this project to quote and reproduce any material posted, in articles or books about the project. I understand that this material will be made anonymous.
- If I am uncomfortable with material after I have posted it, I can contact my local instructor to withdraw my permission to quote or reproduce the material that I have posted.

Please indicate one response:

A: I understand and will follow the guidelines. I give my permission to quote and reproduce material anonymously for educational and research purposes.

B: I do not understand the guidelines and I will ask my local coordinator for help.

C: I do not agree to follow the guidelines. I do not give my permission to quote or reproduce material.

---

**Figure 5.1** Possible template for a 'netiquette' survey and copyright consent

these topics. Chapter 10 gives further advice on addressing problems
that arise during a telecollaboration.

- Promptness of response: Responding promptly is another indication
  of good manners. While it is true that participants in an intercultural
  exchange will not always be available to react to a message as soon
  as it is posted, keeping the conversation going depends on avoid-
  ing long delays in responding to posts. Especially when addressed
  directly, participants should try not to let more than a day pass without responding to a comment or question from one of their partners.

As noted above, these and other possible aspects of 'netiquette' can be
discussed with participants at the beginning of an online exchange. A
template that combines netiquette with copyright permissions is given
in Figure 5.1. It will not be universally applicable; its main function is to
alert the members of the community that their posts should observe community norms of politeness and respect. *How* those norms are construed
and observed will only become apparent once the interactions among
participants begin.

## Security

One of the main concerns in online exchanges is making sure that
participants, especially those who are underage, or minors, remain safe.
Mostly, that means that their personal information will remain private
and that access to participants and interaction with them will remain limited to the telecollaboration. A few simple measures will typically be sufficient for organisers to feel as confident as they can be that the security of
learners is ensured. While some of the actions that can be taken concern
decisions made by the organisers before interaction among participants
begins, others are related to monitoring during the project.

In Chapter 3, we referred to the fact that security should be one of
several factors to consider when choosing the platform on which the
exchange takes place. Security is a problematic issue in the choice of
social media apps as platforms, as they are principally designed for people to find others and connect with them. They also depend financially
on the sharing of user data with third parties. Groups hosted by social
networking companies can be targeted by individuals and companies
who are interested in engaging with certain demographics, but it is possible to minimise that risk. In the past, we have used 'closed' groups on
Facebook as platforms for online exchanges. Since closed group are not
accessible by outside users, they have worked adequately as safe spaces
for interaction. A key consideration is that it should not be possible for
anyone who is not directly associated with the exchange to gain access to
users and their data. Organisers need, therefore, to check the settings on
any social media site they wish to use as a platform.

Some learning management systems give participants a course code requesting access to the online community that is involved in the telecollaboration. Naturally, it is always possible that a participant will share this code with others who are not authorised to join the community. Usually, organisers or instructors will act as online gatekeepers who check requests for access. In all cases, it is imperative that the coordinators of the exchange agree to monitor the list of members and make sure not to accept anyone whose identity is suspect.

When underage participants are expected to join an exchange, extra security measures must be in place. These may include getting written consent from parents or legal guardians before the start of the project, and perhaps even allowing their presence on the platform, with the ability to oversee the interaction, if not to take part in it. While some websites and applications, such as the learning management systems we discussed in Chapter 3, often include that feature, others could make it more difficult to include parents in roles other than as participants.

Explicit authorisations and possibly some form of monitoring from schools may also be required when younger participants are involved. Even when no part of the exchange takes place in actual classrooms, institutions take responsibility for all activities that involve teachers and students, which turns them into stakeholders in the exchange project. Institutional permission might have to be given, and additional assurances will perhaps have to be made in such cases if schools demand them.

## Conclusion

As will be evident from the foregoing discussion, some precautions are more necessary in some educational contexts than in others. While it can be argued that it will be easy for organisers, instructors and participants to agree on basic ethical principles for any intercultural exchange, norms of politeness vary greatly among cultures. The standards for ensuring the security of participants will depend on their age, and the duty of care assumed by any educational institution that safeguards them.

It should be equally clear that ethics, netiquette and security are not marginal concerns in any intercultural exchange. At heart, all three are concerned with right and wrong behaviour. If participants come to believe that their partners are behaving wrongly, or even just inappropriately, then the telecollaboration is likely to be compromised and undermined. However, if organisers and instructors can create a mindset whereby participants believe that their partners are at least trying to observe ethical and polite community norms, any perceived departure from those norms can actually become the subject of intercultural exploration. Needless to say, the security of all participants is an ongoing responsibility of course organisers and instructors. Finally, those organisers and instructors who wish to reuse participants' data in their own research and publications should seek the informed consent of participants and/or those responsible for them.

# 6 Initiating Online Discussions: Breaking the Ice

That the first third of this handbook has been taken up with making preparations for an online exchange indicates how important this phase is in ensuring an effective telecollaboration. However, by this point in the book, we assume that organisers have found willing partners, and agreed on a definition of interculturality, a set of goals, a platform and a means of ensuring the security and reasonable conduct of the participants. The next few chapters consider what actually happens during online intercultural exchanges: how to begin discussions, design more elaborate tasks and build rapport among the participants. We consider how instructors might intervene to support learning, and also when they might have to step in to solve problems that arise among participants. We then consider the assessment of participants' contributions, before looking at how to evaluate the exchange as a whole, and attending to the reuse of learner data, both to promote further learning and to develop an action research project.

The present chapter focuses on ice-breaking and initiating and sustaining discussions. Some telecollaborations may do no more than this: all the authors of this guide have participated in effective online intercultural exchanges that have largely consisted of a series of discussion prompts and responses. As Chapter 7 shows, more elaborate tasks can be designed, but most online intercultural exchanges will include an element of ice-breaking and discussion. Here, then, we consider why ice-breaking remains important in the online world, how instructors and participants might initiate engaging discussions and encourage the crucial step of following up.

## Why are Ice-Breakers Necessary?

It is a common misconception that the online world is qualitatively different from the 'physical' world. It is certainly the case that the online world affords the opportunity to communicate in particular ways. For example, online communicators can conceal their identity behind an avatar, and express ideas that, for whatever reason, they would find difficult to present to a 'live' peer group. If the online discussion is asynchronous, the online communicator also has time to think and craft a considered response to others' messages, in a way that is not always possible in real-time exchanges. However, there are many aspects of online communication that simply replicate or extend certain characteristics of physical communicative events. One such characteristic is the way in which individuals engage with groups of strangers.

Organisers of online intercultural exchanges expect participants in a virtual community to engage in discussion and undertake tasks, and in doing so to build relationships between and across cultural boundaries, in order to learn more about the diverse world in which we live. Participants are expected to learn how to cope constructively with that diversity. In short, organisers expect their learners to enter a space inhabited by a group of people they do not know, with values and beliefs they may or may not share, most of whom will be expressing themselves in a language other than their first language. In that space, participants must build new relationships, with a view to gaining insight into their partners' way of life, thereby gaining new perspectives on their own.

For many individuals, no matter whether or not this process takes place physically or online, there is a considerable challenge simply in establishing a new relationship with a group of strangers. If anything, this challenge is intensified in an online intercultural exchange by the fact that, not only do the members of the group come from different backgrounds and speak different languages, but also they cannot see each other. Some participants will embrace this challenge and participate enthusiastically, while others will exhibit different degrees of shyness. Participants will inevitably use the initial contributions to any exchange, consciously or unconsciously, to make assessments about their new partners' character and language ability. It will be clear, then, that organisers and instructors cannot simply set up a platform, put participants in touch with each other and expect successful interactions to naturally follow.

In many respects, then, the challenge for instructors in initiating communication in a new online intercultural exchange is similar to that facing instructors when they begin to teach a new language class. Classroom teachers need to prompt learners' contributions, at the very start, with the primary goal of building learners' confidence in themselves and developing their trust in each other. In a 'physical' classroom, activities designed to build confidence and trust at the start of a course of study are usually called 'ice-breakers' or 'warm-ups'. For the same reasons, ice-breakers are necessary when starting an online intercultural exchange. They allow participants to become familiar with the platform and their partners, and to begin to imagine their own place within the online community.

## What Should Ice-Breakers Do?

As Rojas Giraldo (2021) has demonstrated, the main purpose of ice-breakers, generally, in language education, is to establish and promote group cohesion. In an online exchange, their principal aim is to establish connections and arouse curiosity among participants by inviting them to display and respond to aspects of their personal background and preferences. By making these connections visible, the ice-breakers should establish empathy and trust, and open up avenues for further exploration. The function of ice-breakers is also to reduce participants' anxiety about communicating with each other through the target language, or languages, and to lay the basis for further – and deeper – communication in the future. Ice-breakers also establish *rapport*, which, as it is something that pervades all online communication, is treated more fully in Chapter 8.

In her extensive study of the function of ice-breakers, Rojas Giraldo draws on the literature of social cohesion to identify what set of attitudes the ice-breakers aim to promote. She also considers the kinds of communicative activity that can be devised to help form these attitudes. An effective group, which for the present purposes is an effective online community, should develop the following characteristics (cf. Rojas Giraldo, 2021: 35):

- A unified perception of the group as a stable, organic whole.
- A desire to engage with other members of the group (social cohesion).
- A commitment to the tasks that group members are required to address (task cohesion).
- A sense of satisfaction or pride in being a member of the group.

The ways in which instructors describe the community, and the ice-breakers that instructors design to introduce participants to each other, should all have the aim of developing these characteristics. The instructors need to present participants with a clear and attractive description of the community, and to try to instil a sense of satisfaction in being a community member. The ice-breakers themselves will also seek to promote these characteristics. At the outset, participants will exhibit differing degrees of social and task cohesion, and so the ice-breakers should actively encourage all participants to contribute. It is likely that online communities with a relatively small and stable membership will develop closer bonds. Larger online communities, in which participants come and go, will present more challenges for the instructors.

## Effective Ice-Breakers

Effective ice-breakers allow participants to engage in a display of their own identity, and in an exploration of the identity of others. In saying this, we are not suggesting that learners have a pre-established identity that is 'reflected' in their posts; we take the view that learners' identity is at least in part co-constructed during and by their interactions. Even so, learners will draw on aspects of their past life and experiences to present a public face to fellow members of the group. Group cohesion, then, will, in part, be affected by (i) the similarities they find in the posts of fellow group members; (ii) whether or not they find any differences among themselves complementary to their own identities or completely alien to their interests; and (iii) whether or not they find the posts and responses of other group members (which may indicate similarity, complementarity or strangeness) stimulating or engaging. One of the challenges for organisers is to support the development of group cohesion in circumstances in which group members do *not* find each other's identity engaging (see further below). Effective ice-breakers, then, will do some of the following (cf. Rojas Giraldo, 2021: 38):

- Allow group members to learn about each other.
- Encourage regular interaction as well as the display of individual identity.
- Encourage cooperation in shared tasks.
- Prompt the sharing of similar experiences.
- Begin to develop a group history and ethos.

The kinds of effective ice-breaker that are familiar to many teachers in the physical classroom clearly address these aims; ice-breakers for online intercultural exchange should attempt to achieve similar ends.

## Instructor-Generated Ice-Breakers

Ice-breakers are naturally associated with the start of courses or exchanges, when there is a pressing need to establish a positive group identity. However, ice-breakers are also recommended for later moments in an exchange when group cohesion seems to be weakening and needs to be re-energised, or otherwise attended to. Examples of simple online ice-breaking activities that address these aims include the following. Not all of them will be equally effective.

(1) Write a personal profile, with information such as name, nationality, country and place of residence, hobbies, plans for the future and reasons for learning the target language.
(2) Introduce yourself briefly and write down five words that best describe you.
(3) Find a group member who plays a sport, plays a musical instrument, has a pet, prefers coffee to tea, goes regularly to the cinema, can speak three different languages, uses languages for work/study, etc.

(4) If you could buy one famous painting to hang in your home, what would it be – and why?

(5) What is on your 'bucket list' (that is, a list of things you want to do before you 'kick the bucket' or die)?

All of these ice-breakers could conceivably attend to the building of group cohesion, although some might be considered more suited to certain groups than others (e.g. adult professionals versus teens). The first on the list might work well in online communities with a high sense of task cohesion, but the ice-breaker itself is not particularly engaging. It presents participants with information about their partners that might indicate similarity, complementarity or strangeness (perhaps particularly in the question about hobbies and plans for the future) but it is largely predicated on facts rather than feelings.

The second ice-breaker on the list offers more opportunity to display emotion and individuality. There is still room for expression of the basic facts about a participant, but the 'five words that best describe you' are less predictable, prompt affective as well as factual responses, and are thus potentially more open to further exploration. With the instructor's encouragement, this ice-breaker might prompt more engaged social interaction among participants.

The third ice-breaker is a variant of the first on the list, except that it encourages interaction rather than a monologic display of individual identity. Rather than simply telling fellow participants about oneself and waiting for a follow-up, each participant has to use the platform to find information about the others. This is a more engaging ice-breaker than the first, but demands a higher degree of social confidence and linguistic competence than the simple display of one's own individual characteristics.

The final two examples of ice-breakers focus less on the factual profile of the participants, and more on their tastes. The fourth ice-breaker assumes at least a minimal knowledge of and interest in the visual arts – and the willingness of participants to interrogate each other's preferences and justify their own. If successful, however, this ice-breaker could be informative and generate social bonds among participants who might find each other's choices similar to their own, complementary or unusual. It can easily be adapted to taste in music, film or television. The final example speaks to the peculiar fascination that many participants in online discussion groups have with lists (e.g. 'my top 10 best films of all time'), but it also elicits preferences that construct an identity for public consumption. Again, fellow participants might find each other's choices similar to their own, complementary or simply strange or unknown. A sample of participant responses to an ice-breaking task is given in the next section.

## Learner Responses

The particular context for this example of an ice-breaker is an edition of an ongoing, annual, informal, online intercultural exchange, 'The Hemispheres Connection' run by a group of colleagues in different countries (Lima & Dart, 2019). The exchange is informal in that it has been run as a voluntary, extra-curricular activity, rather than as a specific class project. In this particular edition, the countries involved were Argentina, Brazil, China, Greece and Israel. The age of the participants ranged from 14 to late 20s, and they were arranged by the organisers into two groups by age: roughly 14–20 and then 20 upwards. To break the ice in the first week, the task shown in Figure 6.1 was posted by John Corbett, one of the organisers and instructors. It offers information (thus modelling possible language) and then elicits comparable information from the participants. It has some unanswered questions that are designed to invite follow-up questions by the participants questions. It also attempts to generate a sense of excitement about the project in the hope that participants will feel engaged and motivated.

This ice-breaker prompted a number of responses, three of which are shown in Figure 6.2. The names of the participants have been changed, but otherwise the posts are unaltered.

To be able to respond, even in a basic way, to the ice-breaking prompt, the participants need to be able to talk about their name, the seasons of the year, their hobbies and travel preferences. The responses in Figure 6.2 show different levels of English, but all are potentially good responses to the instructor's prompt in that they offer opportunities for developing group cohesion and intercultural exploration. That is, their responses indicate areas of commonality, complementarity and

---

My name's John and I teach at United International College, in Zhuhai. I am originally from Scotland, but I actually live in Brazil. And I work in China... I've lived and worked in various places: Italy, Russia, Canada, the UK, Macau and now China. I'm entering my seventh decade (!)

I am professionally interested in English language teaching and intercultural communication. But I am personally interested in travel, food, Scottish literature, movies... I don't have a nickname now, but when I was a child at school, I was called 'Corbie'. It shortens my surname (Corbett) but it also has a particular meaning in the Scots language.

That's me. Now please tell us a little about you!

- What is your name and your nickname (if you have one – what does it mean)?
- How old are you?
- Have you got a hobby or favourite pastime? What is it?
- What is your favourite season of the year – and why?
- Where would you like to travel?

Please answer these questions in this discussion area, and also please comment and ask questions about the posts of others. Let's start some conversations. If you have more questions for me, do please ask!

We all have a brilliant journey ahead. Fasten your seat belts, friends!

---

**Figure 6.1** A sample ice-breaker

Participant response 1: China

Hello! I'm Lestlin. Maybe you will think this is a weird name, but actually each letter in this name stands for a words which is important to me. I'm 17, a year one student in university. I'm a great fan of music and I love singing! I love autumn the best because of the temperature is just fine for me to live and in China there will be lots of holidays. If I have the chance, I would like to travel to Korea because the food there is great and my idol also lives there. Hope we can get along well!

Participant response 2: Brazil

Hello everyone! My name is Eloisa, I don't really have a nickname, so you can call me just Eloisa! I am from Brazil and live in the city of Rio de Janeiro, the one with the big statue called Christ the Redeemer. I am currently 15 years old, but my 16th birthday is in a week 😊. My favorite pastime is dancing, I like to search choreographies on-line and try to learn them. I also like to learn new languages and I am currently trying to teach myself french! My favorite season of the year is spring. Summers here in Brazil are very hot, with temperatures higher than 33°C, so I prefer spring, because it's not that hot and we can enjoy the day outside. My dream is to travel all around the world, but if I were to choose it would be France, Italy or Korea! France and Italy, because I love the vibe from their cities, languages they speak and their culture. Korea, because it seams like a very fun place and rich of culture, from what I can see through K-pop and K-dramas. My next trip will probably be to Portugal though, since my family is planing on moving there and I am very exited! Thank you guys for reading! I can't wait to read your answers and to get to know you!

Participant response 3: Israel

hi everyone my name is Jamila, and my family call me jami, I'm 22 ears old and I'm a forth year student at the Arab Academic college of education in Haifa, I study English because I loved English since I was young.

I love to read, journal and to embroidery.

winter is my favorite season because I love cold weather and the rain.

I would like to travel to London.

**Figure 6.2** Participant responses

difference that might be explored further. The participants show differing degrees of formality of greeting and a sense of community, tending towards the informal ('Hello/Hello everyone/hi everyone') and two conclude their posts with 'leave-taking' formulae ('Hope we can get along well!' and 'I can't wait to read your answers and get to know you'). In class debriefings in each location, even these basic elements of the posts can be reflected on: what kinds of language do participants in China, Brazil and Israel feel are more or less appropriate to the interaction?

The content of the posts is also worth reflecting on in class. The participants' stance towards naming practices differs: Lestlin chose her name according to the significance of the letters; Eloisa has no nickname; and Jamila's is simply a diminutive of her full name, used by her family. They are all students with different seasonal preferences (autumn, spring and winter) but a common dislike of weather that is too hot. They have different hobbies (e.g. singing, dancing, embroidery), but two have common travel preferences: both Lestlin and Eloisa are interested in Korea, and both indicate the current reach and popularity of Korean popular culture. The responses, then, show potential for a more extensive discussion of each other's opening response. To do this properly, however, the participants need to be prepared to follow up their initial contribution, and to follow up effectively.

## The Importance of Follow-Up

As we have seen, the initial responses to the ice-breakers show participants beginning to co-construct an identity in relation to their fellow community members. The issue of participant identity and how it is negotiated online is discussed in more detail in Chapter 8. For the moment, the main issue is that participants reveal facts about themselves that might form the basis for more extensive interactions. Let us now consider how one of these posts was followed up.

There were three follow-ups to Lestlin's opening response (Figure 6.3). Two pick up on her interest in the Korean language and culture, and one picks up on the meaning of her unusual name, asking if it is common Chinese practice to make an English name out of the initial letters of significant words. Lestlin responds to each follow-up question, although to none in its entirety, leaving unmentioned the level of difficulty Chinese learners have in mastering Korean script and leaving open the actual meaning of her name – and so the discussion thread ends. There is no further query, for example about Lee Dong Wook, Lestlin's 'idol', although, of course, those who are interested might now look him up on the internet.

---

Melina (from Corfu)

Hello!! You've said you are from China, right? I was always wondering whether it's difficult for someone who speaks Chinese to learn Korean or the opposite. Do you generally find it hard to learn the Korean writing system??

Maria Fernanda (from Brazil)

Hi Lestlin!! You said that one of the reasons of you wanting to visit Korea is your idol living there... Now I'm curious... Who is your idol??

Lestlin

Actually my idol is Lee Dong Wook. And For me Korean is not that hard to learn because there are lots of words which come from Chinese and the pronunciation is very similar

Rodrigo (from Brazil)

Hello Lestlin! I really don't want to offend or disrespect, I'm just curious. You said that each letter on your name (Lestlin) has a meaning, they represent a different word, right? So, in the Chinese culture, do people are usually named using this 'method'? And also, China use a different alphabet, right? Would Lestlin be a translation then? If yes, how is your name in your language?

Thank you.

Lestlin

Each letter in my name stands for a English words, and you can guess what are they!

---

**Figure 6.3** Follow-up questions and responses

The interaction in Figure 6.3, modest though it may be, succeeds in 'breaking the ice' in that it engages Lestlin at least in minimal interaction with participants from Greece and Brazil. For further interaction to have taken place, Lestlin might have had to be more explicit in inviting further follow-ups in her responses, for example by asking Melina or Maria Fernanda what their knowledge of or interest in Korea might be.

It is also unclear whether Lestlin is genuinely inviting participants to guess the meaning of her name or if she is unwilling to reveal information that is personal to her. At this stage in the interaction, her fellow participants might have felt that to take the invitation at face value would have been intrusive. That said, Lestlin's responses to the follow-ups are typical of participant engagement at this early stage in online exchanges, and similar examples can be used in initial in-class reflections as part of classroom discussions on how to elicit longer and fuller interactions.

### Participant-Generated Ice-Breakers

There are many ways in which even ice-breakers can go wrong. As soon as participants begin constructing an identity, by revealing some aspect of their experiences, beliefs, attitudes, tastes and desires for group consumption, they leave themselves open to potentially unwanted interrogation and even mockery. Although the norms of 'netiquette' will have been set out in advance (see Chapter 5), once actual interaction starts, the apparent boundaries between appropriate and inappropriate interaction can become blurred. This is evident in Figure 6.3 when Rodrigo carefully frames his question about Lestlin's name with 'I really don't want to offend or disrespect, I'm just curious'. It is important that organisers check that participants are able to articulate such frames so that they can negotiate topics that might be difficult (see further, Chapter 10).

In most circumstances, however, the worst that can happen is that participants fail to engage in interaction. This can be seen in the discussion thread in Figure 6.4, which shows two follow-ups (by the Brazilians, Rodrigo and Eloisa) to a post by a younger group member (the Argentinian, Claudia). Claudia's post addresses the prompts in the ice-breaking task, identifying two 'passions': a favourite season and a preferred travel destination. The two Brazilian participants follow up the post by picking up on Claudia's favourite season, winter. Rodrigo asks an explicit question, focusing on the different seasons in which Christmas occurs north and south of the equator, while Eloisa gives information about Christmas in Natal (a city whose name, translated into English, literally means 'Christmas'). Claudia does not follow up either response.

We have no information about why Claudia did not follow up the responses, and there might have been, obviously, any number of reasons why she did not do so. However, in our experience, one common observation about instructors' prompts, given by participants in online

---

Claudia (from Argentina)

My name is Claudia and I am fourteen years old. I have two hobbies. The first one is dance and the other one is make up. These two are my passion.
My favourite season of the year is winter, because we celebrate Christmas and I like to see things with all the lights and also because it is my birthday. I would love to travel to US, because all the skyscrapers, the people and all the fashion is iconic.

Rodrigo (from Brazil)

Hello Claudia! You said you like winter because of Christmas, right? In Brazil we have Christmas on summer. It's kind of sad for me sometimes because I think the lights and all other Christimas' decorations are even more beautiful when it's snowing. We don't have snow in Rio de Janeiro either, but I can see online pictures of it. Where do you live ? Do you have snow there?

Eloisa (from Brazil)

Hi Claudia, you said you like christmas, I am from Brazil and I live in a sunny city called 'Natal', if I translate into English it means Christmas, we have a catchphrase that says 'Christmas in Christmas'😊 at this time of year the city is busier than usual because it joins the summer season

---

**Figure 6.4** Unresponsive participants

exchanges, is their perceived 'inauthenticity'. That is, the tasks given by the instructors, such as the ice-breaker in Figure 6.1, are designed primarily as language exercises and not as genuine conversation openers. If that were the case, it might simply be the fact that Rodrigo and Eloisa found themselves asking Claudia about a topic – her favourite season – in which she had, in fact, little personal interest. She was simply dutifully responding to a language exercise and had little motivation to extend the interaction further.

One of the most frustrating aspects of online exchanges for participants is to write posts that are not responded to. When this happens, motivation swiftly declines. One advantage of ice-breakers is that they can diagnose whether participants in the community are likely to be genuinely engaged contributors (like Eloisa and Rodrigo) or not (like Claudia). At an early stage, in an in-class debriefing on the responses and follow-ups to the previous week's ice-breaker, issues of responsiveness can be raised and discussed. As noted, it may well be that participants observe that the prompt itself was simply unengaging.

One way of addressing the perceived 'inauthenticity' of discussion prompts given by instructors is to elicit potential topics from the students themselves. Before posting the prompt online, there can be a period of rehearsal during class time, in which participants themselves are asked what they are interested in. Alternatively, the 'inauthentic' nature of instructors' prompts may become a topic of class discussion, with the instructors inviting participants to draft and try out prompts that satisfy their genuine curiosity. In our experience, participants often come up with topics that the instructors would not have imagined being of interest. What will spark participants' genuine curiosity clearly varies from exchange to exchange, but among the most successful discussion prompts

- Mitigation strategy (e.g, 'I know it's a stupid/silly/obvious/etc question but...')
- The question to be asked (e.g. '...what is your favourite non-alcoholic drink?')
- An expression of genuine personal interest in the topic (e.g. 'I am really curious to know.')
- A personal statement on the topic (e.g. 'Mine would have to be that old favourite, tea. I know other people prefer coffee, but for me you can't beat a good cuppa tea!')
- Elicitation of response (e.g. 'Looking forward to your responses!')

**Figure 6.5** Generic formula for participant-generated ice-breakers/discussion prompts

that we have encountered are those that were participant generated, e.g. 'What is your favourite non-alcoholic drink?' or 'How do people where you live commemorate those who have died, serving their country in war?'.

The participants who drafted prompts offered their own responses to them ('milk, straight from the cow'; 'poppies') and then elicited further responses from the online community. Such participant-generated discussion prompts have resulted in the most extensive and interesting threads that we have encountered over the years. In-class rehearsals can thus elicit possible ice-breakers and discussion prompts from participants. A tested generic 'formula' for such ice-breakers is shown in Figure 6.5 (cf. Corbett & Phipps, 2006: 167).

The generic 'formula' can be discussed in a class briefing and different questions evaluated as, for example, 'strange' or 'silly' or 'obvious'. There are obviously different ways of mitigating the question to be asked, expressing personal interest and eliciting responses. In-class discussions can focus on expanding the participants' linguistic repertoire in this respect.

## Conclusion

This chapter has focused on the key initial phase of an online intercultural exchange, one in which the instructors set a task (written by themselves and/or participants) that prompts a discussion whose primary purpose is to generate a sense of organic community, get to know the diverse membership and raise motivation. More important than the participants' replies to the instructor's prompts are their follow-up responses to each other. Responses to the ice-breakers, or discussion prompts can also provide useful material for an initial debriefing session in class, which may address issues of participation, appropriate language and behaviour, and levels of engagement with the exchange. The next chapters focus on the design of more elaborate intercultural tasks and the management of rapport.

# 7 Designing Online Intercultural Tasks

Chapter 6 described ice-breaking activities and discussion prompts that are largely designed to establish a sense of community identity and solidarity among participants. While some online intercultural exchanges can consist entirely of a series of ice-breakers and discussion prompts, others may require participants to engage in more elaborate tasks, or tasks focused on particular themes. This chapter considers the design of online tasks that seek to enhance participants' sense of interculturality, or aspects of their intercultural communicative competence. It reviews the nature of tasks that are designed with intercultural goals in mind, summarises the basic components of the intercultural communicative task and provides a detailed illustration of a possible ethnographic task that can be used as a model or template for others.

## What are Online Intercultural Tasks?

Organisers and instructors of intercultural telecollaborations face the challenge of designing tasks that can be used to explore culture through online exchanges. Given the breadth of the concept of 'culture', the advice given here can by no means be comprehensive, nor will it cover all the types of tasks that can be designed for a successful online exchange. O'Dowd (2012: 345–347) lists a number of task types, beyond informal discussions, that have been used in different telecollaborations to explore participants' cultural experiences:

- Authoring 'cultural autobiographies'.
- Carrying out virtual interviews.
- Exchanging story collections.
- Comparing parallel texts, e.g. common folk tales or remakes of films.
- Comparing class questionnaires.
- Analysing cultural products, e.g. films, literature, pieces of material culture.
- Collaborative translation activities.

- Collaborative creation of a product such as an essay or PowerPoint presentation.
- Rewriting of texts from one genre to another.
- Collaboration in 'closed outcome' activities such as 'spot the differences' pictures.
- Making cultural translations/adaptations, e.g. revising a film scene or an advertisement from one culture so that it is appropriate for another.

This list illustrates the range of activities that might be included in an online intercultural exchange, or, indeed, that might become the basis of a particular telecollaboration. Some telecollaborations can take the form of an online film or book club, for example.

Different activity types can make lesser or greater linguistic and intercultural demands on participants. As O'Dowd acknowledges, some activities are more suitable for some online communities than others, and all have their strengths and weaknesses. For example, participants can be encouraged to write an autobiography for display to the community, or they might be required to interview a fellow participant, in order to write a profile that will be shared online. Both activities are challenging and may be engaging; however, in some circumstances, each might lead to cultural stereotyping. The guidance given in this chapter is therefore quite general in that it applies to the design of many of the task types that O'Dowd describes, by breaking down the components of the intercultural communicative task, and considering each aspect in turn (cf. Corbett, 2022: 73–77).

## Defining Intercultural Goals

In Chapter 1, we suggested some characteristics of intercultural communicative competence that organisers and instructors might use in initial discussions about the intended goals of the telecollaboration. It follows that organisers and instructors have to reach a consensus on what makes a communicative task intercultural. A succinct response is that it is a task that requires participants to deploy their linguistic repertoire in such a way that they demonstrate their capacity to be effective explorers and interpreters of both familiar and unfamiliar cultures (cf. Belz, 2007; O'Dowd & Dooly, 2020). By completing the task successfully, the repertoire will be strengthened or enhanced.

However, this response begs several questions, not least of which is how 'familiar and unfamiliar cultures' might be defined. The likely nature of many online intercultural exchanges – namely, that they involve participants of different nationalities, from different countries – might encourage a relatively conservative view of culture as being based on nationality. However, the process of interacting with participants from other countries will usually show other cultural categories emerging, e.g. cultures based on age, gender, profession, faith, socioeconomic background and hobbies (cf. Risager, 2007). The dialogue between Eloisa and Lestlin reported in Chapter 6 shows a young Brazilian and a young Chinese participant sharing a cultural interest in and knowledge of Korean popular culture, for example. This shared interest bonds them into a 'youth' category that potentially distinguishes them from 'typical' older Chinese and Brazilian consumers of popular culture. Similarly, school pupils might share more attitudes, beliefs and values with fellow school pupils across national boundaries than they do with university students or working adults in their own countries.

The 'exploration and interpretation of culture', then, requires participants to be alert to different aspects of similarity and difference that bond individuals into diverse kinds of collective. Lestlin and Eloisa might belong to different national cultures, but they also belong to similar cultures in respect of their age, gender and taste in the products of popular music culture. Intercultural communicative competence can be understood as a construct that attempts to describe the ability of individuals such as Lestlin and Eloisa to draw on their communicative resources to explore, interpret and negotiate these points of divergence and contact.

The construct of intercultural communicative competence, as it has been developed over the past four decades, still attracts lively debate (e.g. Dervin, 2012; Dervin & Gross, 2016). As we have already mentioned, transnational curricular documents such as the *Common European Framework of Reference* (*CEFR*; Council of Europe, 2001; North et al., 2018) and the North American National Council of State Supervisors for Languages–American Council on the Teaching of Foreign Languages 'can do' statements (NCSSFL-ACTFL, 2017a, 2017b) attempt to describe intercultural communicative competence not only as a set of linguistic resources but also as attitudes such as curiosity and openness, and personal qualities such as the resilience required to cope with culture shock.

Problems undoubtedly arise if such constructs are treated uncritically. For example, there is the questionable implication that attitudes such as 'curiosity' and 'openness' are positive cultural universals, and that they find expression in similar ways across languages. There is also anxiety that what might in fact be a fluid and holistic repertoire of linguistic and personal resources is distorted by the reductive attempt to atomise it as a definite and static set of abstract universal qualities. Even so, if treated with caution, the descriptions of intercultural communicative competence offered by documents such as the *CEFR* and the NCSSFL-ACTFL 'can-do' statements provide useful guidance for those designing tasks for online intercultural exchanges. Caution demands that the organisers and instructors of intercultural exchanges treat the outcome of the tasks with the kind of openness they demand of their participants. Intercultural communicative competence may well lie not so much in the development of a set of abilities that ensure intercultural communication goes well, but in the development of strategies that enable individuals to cope effectively and resiliently, and adapt, when communication does not go well.

## The Components of Intercultural Tasks

The designer of tasks for online intercultural exchanges can draw on a consensus, established over the past 50 years about how foreign languages are best taught and learned, namely by regularly engaging learners in tasks that demand that they deploy and enhance their linguistic resources. Designers of tasks for online intercultural exchanges, then, can turn to familiar resources such as Nunan (1989, 2004) which suggest that acquisition happens when learners are using the target language to accomplish something that is meaningful to them. The object for the organisers of online intercultural exchanges is to persuade participants that the tasks they are being presented with are meaningful, and then to 'scaffold' the process of online exchange so that the learners enhance their linguistic repertoire to the point where they feel they are satisfied with the nature of their interactions (for a further discussion of scaffolding, see Chapter 9).

Nunan (1989: 10–11) presents a simple, comprehensive model of the communicative task (Figure 7.1) that is useful for organisers of online intercultural exchanges. The ice-breaking activities suggested in Chapter 6 can be evaluated with reference to this model, and it also provides a template for the design of more extensive activities such as those suggested by O'Dowd (2012), listed at the start of this chapter. The various elements of the communicative task, as presented by Nunan, are discussed, one by one, in the following sections, with particular reference to the design of online tasks for intercultural exchange.

## Goals

As we observed in the preceding section, the goal of intercultural tasks is broadly to develop intercultural communicative competence. That is, part of the broad goal is to enhance each participant's linguistic repertoire, and another part is to engage participants in tasks that activate socially valued attitudes and personal qualities that might be described as curiosity, empathy, open-mindedness, resilience, self-awareness, humility, respect, tact, generosity, hospitality, criticality and

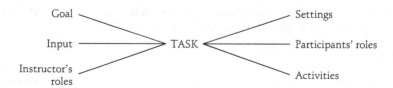

**Figure 7.1**  Elements of the communicative task (cf. Nunan, 1989: 10–11)

so on. Again, we bear in mind that these qualities might be realised in different ways across different cultures.

Less broadly, the goals of online intercultural exchanges can be defined as focusing on the observation, description, interpretation, comparison and constructively critical evaluation of different cultural patterns of language and behaviour, both familiar and unfamiliar. This process of observation, description, interpretation, comparison and evaluation demands of participants two general sets of skills, which can be categorised as ethnographic and semiotic (cf. Corbett, 2022; Roberts *et al.*, 2001). In short, the tasks developed for online intercultural exchanges focus on aspects of observation and description (ethnography) and interpretation (semiotics) as the basis for comparison and evaluation. Simply put, tasks can encourage participants individually and in collaboration to notice things, describe things, discuss the possible meanings of things, compare things and evaluate things. Participants will need to develop a linguistic repertoire to enable them to achieve these goals.

The activities suggested by O'Dowd (2012) and listed at the outset of this chapter can be related wholly or partially to these goals. For instance, the 'cultural autobiography' involves noticing and selecting events from one's past experience that are considered interesting enough to describe to others. The autobiographies then become the basis for interpretation, comparison and evaluation in an online discussion. The instructors' role is to stimulate, support and moderate the description and discussion. Similarly, 'analysing cultural products' involves observing and describing incidents from films, novels, stories, songs or advertisements across cultures that can then be interpreted, compared and evaluated. The instructors' task is to design a procedure for participants to try to ensure that all these stages are accomplished. 'Collaborative creation of a product' may be less easy to relate to these goals, as the nature of the task will depend in part on the product being created. However, if participants are jointly involved in producing, say, tourist guides to each other's place of residence, then they will all need to notice and describe possible attractions, compare them, interpret their significance to locals and outsiders, and evaluate their merit or otherwise for inclusion in the final product.

The sample tasks illustrated later in this chapter can also be related to the intercultural goals of noticing, describing, interpreting, comparing and evaluating. Again, these goals also have linguistic correlates in that participants will need sufficient language resources to describe, interpret, compare and evaluate, and to negotiate their interpretations and evaluations within the community. One key decision is when and how to introduce such language (see section titled 'Instructor's Roles').

## Input

The *input* to an online intercultural exchange refers to whatever material prompts participants to interact. In ice-breakers, the input might be instructor-generated or participant-generated prompts for discussion. However, as we have seen, the input to more extensive tasks can include cultural products such as websites, advertisements, literature, films and television programmes or video clips. Input can also be descriptions of the past experiences of participants, as recounted in autobiographies or negotiated in interviews.

Corbett (2010) offers a set of practical ethnographic tasks for English language learning, many of which can be used in or adapted for online intercultural exchanges. The input for many of these tasks is everyday life, in that participants are invited to observe aspects of their daily routines and describe them as a basis for presentation to and discussion with others. These tasks are particularly designed to develop 'noticing' skills, and the linguistic repertoires of description and presentation. An alternative way of using everyday life as input is described by Alareer *et al.* (2022) in their account of an online intercultural exchange between university students in Gaza, Palestine, and Natal in Brazil. Students there turned their daily experiences of conflict and marginalisation into creative writing and 'flash non-fiction' (that is, short vignettes based on observations of everyday life) for presentation and discussion by their telecollaborators.

Input, ultimately, is the prompt for the online task. Other participants and their accounts of everyday life may function as the raw input for ethnographic tasks; cultural products such as news sites, films and literature can be the input for more interpretive or semiotic tasks. The question then arises as to what participants are expected to do with the input (see section titled 'Activities').

## Instructor's Roles

While there might have been, in the early days of telecollaboration, a popular misconception that online exchanges would run themselves, the various roles of the organiser and instructor are still fundamental to their success (see further, Chapter 9). Instructors remain crucial to the organisation and sequencing of tasks, even if these responsibilities are shared with fellow instructors and the participants themselves. They are directly involved in the selection and design of tasks, the presentation of language, overseeing any rehearsals, giving advice, monitoring task procedures, prompting discussion and delivering feedback.

While instructors' responsibilities are varied, there is often a question of how closely they should be involved in the actual task procedures. For example, in 'ice-breaking' discussions, should instructors or organisers offer their own views or evaluate participants' contributions directly online? Views on this question are mixed. In some exchanges, participants enjoy the relative freedom to articulate their own views without instructors' intervention. In other exchanges, participants are keen to hear their instructors' own perspective on the tasks given. In most exchanges, participants will hold a variety of views about the role of the instructors. It is therefore advisable that the instructors' role also be a matter for explicit discussion with participants. Whatever the outcome of such discussions, organisers and instructors of online intercultural exchanges should seek to demonstrate tact, giving participants space to develop their own ideas, and eliciting views rather than evaluating. That said, instructors might also have the responsibility of intervening if controversial or difficult subject matters are raised in the online exchange (see further, Chapter 10).

## Settings

In the traditional, physical language classroom, settings are relatively straightforward: tasks can involve learners working individually, in pairs, in groups or as a class. Each type of setting has its affordances: individual work can encourage reflection and consolidation of learning, pair work allows intensive practice of recently presented language items, and group work might require that learners draw on their fuller repertoire of language or languages in order to accomplish a task. Whole-class work might involve the teacher presenting new language, explaining procedures before the task is attempted and eliciting feedback or leading discussion once it is completed.

When the learning space is extended online, the settings become more complex. Added to the 'physical' settings are different possibilities for participants to work in pairs or groups with online telecollaborators. Online partners might interview each other or they might work together to complete a shared task. While these settings clearly offer rich potential for the learning of language and culture, they might equally be frustrating for participants who are paired with partners who do not meet their expectations in terms of responsiveness. As noted earlier in this volume (Chapter 4), this issue can be anticipated and addressed to some extent by agreeing on expectations in advance of the project. However, working with partners online is demanding for many participants in online intercultural exchanges, and the risks of disappointment can be reduced by, for example, creating trust at the start of the online relationship, by involving online partners in less demanding tasks, and by requiring online partners to work in groups rather than pairs, with certain participants specifically nominated to monitor the frequency of interaction.

## Participants' Roles

The demands on participants, usually language learners, in online intercultural exchanges, are also varied and considerable. Individuals are required to move into a virtual space occupied by peers with different levels of language proficiency and from quite different cultural backgrounds, and they need to engage in discussions or accomplish tasks according to a given or negotiated syllabus. They have to develop, as the discussion in Chapter 6 puts it, 'social and task cohesion', that is, they need to display motivation to contribute in a responsible way to the development of the online community and engage with others in accomplishing the tasks. The development of social and task cohesion can again be supported by an explicit statement at the outset of the exchange about the expectations of community members, but it needs to be supported also by the staging of tasks and feedback supplied by the instructors.

Throughout the course, participants will be expected to internalise and use new language to accomplish the tasks given, to develop social skills for online partnership and to display aspects of intercultural communicative competence, such as curiosity, respect, openness and humility. Humility, in this context, can be understood as a willingness to reappraise oneself, a positive orientation towards otherness, a predilection towards working constructively with others, the ability to manage one's own emotions and an appreciation of the value of everyday phenomena (cf. Paine et al., 2016: 15).

There is an ongoing debate about whether these mooted characteristics of interculturality are 'taught or caught', that is, whether the tasks assigned in intercultural exchanges actually develop intercultural communicative competence, or whether they simply allow space for those who are predisposed to be interculturally competent to demonstrate that competence. Corbett and Phipps (2006) conclude that even if the activities that are required by online intercultural exchanges merely give a space for participants to demonstrate their pre-existing intercultural competence, there is still a value in activating their curiosity, respect, humility and so on, and reflecting on these characteristics as a basis for effective interaction across and between cultures.

## Activities

The activities used in any online intercultural exchange can be quite varied. Participants can initiate discussions in response to the ice-breakers and prompts described in Chapter 6, or they can be asked to undertake more elaborate activities that involve noticing, describing, presenting, comparing and evaluating. Such activities might include:

- Visit a local place that you like, and note what you see, hear, smell, touch and taste there. Write a description either as a short paragraph or a poem. Be prepared to share it with members of the online exchange community.
- Visit a neighbourhood café and describe the décor and products available. Describe the customers and watch the interactions between them and the staff members. Present your description online.

Compare cafés in the localities represented by participants in the online community.

- Interview street artists (e.g. buskers, 'standing statues' and jugglers) about their performances and their daily lives. Present your findings online and compare street art around the localities represented by the community.
- Take photographs of the 'linguistic landscape' of public signs in your locality (e.g. shop signs, official notices, graffiti, advertisements), focusing on signage in different languages. Compare signage across the online community.
- Take a photograph of an important item of furniture in your home (e.g. the kitchen table, a sofa, a cabinet that displays ornaments or photos, the television). Describe where in the house this item of furniture is, how it is used by you and the family and why it is important to you.
- Visit a public event (e.g. a sports game, a service in a religious institution, a parade or celebration). Describe carefully what you observe. If you can, interview some of the participants and find out what the event means to them. Do some research into the history of the event (e.g. the history of the game and the teams observed, the history of the religion and the local institution, the history of the festival or celebration) and present your findings online for discussion.

From the above examples, it will be evident that many intercultural activities for online exchanges consist of project-based tasks that are designed both to enhance language proficiency and develop skills in practical ethnography and critical thinking (cf. Corbett, 2010, 2022). When designing such tasks, it is useful to think of both the language focus and the desired aspect of intercultural competence that is to be addressed. When considering appropriate tasks, the instructors might sketch out an outline summary, the intercultural focus, the language level expected of the participants, how long the activities are expected to last and whether or not in-class preparation is required beforehand. If in-class preparation is required, instructors might note down the procedure for presenting the task to the participants. For participants who are still developing the skills of ethnographic observation, the instructors might design a 'schedule' that guides their observations. A detailed example of one such extended activity and an observation schedule is provided in Figure 7.2.

## A Sample Activity: Exploring Public Spaces

*Outline*: This activity encourages participants to explore public space in their own culture. They will choose a public space to observe and describe, and then compare notes with members of the online community.

> **Observation schedule**
>
> Time and location:
> Type of activity:
> Describe the people who were involved:
> How were they dressed?
> How did they communicate with each other?
> What kind of things did they say?
> What kind of behaviour was expected or allowed?
> What kind of behaviour was not allowed?

**Figure 7.2** Observation schedule for intercultural activity

*Focus*: To observe, describe, reflect on and compare interactions in a chosen public space.

*Level*: Intermediate and above.

*Time*: 30 to 40 minutes in the first lesson; 90 minutes outside class to do the observation; 40 minutes in the second lesson to prepare a presentation to be posted online. Then 30 to 60 minutes to follow up and discuss other participants' presentations.

*Preparation*: The procedure suggested below can be adapted to the needs of different groups of participants. This activity involves participants visiting a public place (individually, in pairs or in groups) in their own time and reporting their observations to the class – and then to their partners online.

*Procedure*:

(1) Explain that the participants, individually, in pairs or in groups, are going to explore a public place of their choice, observe the behaviour and interactions that take place there, and then report their findings to the class and then to their online partners.

(2) Brainstorm with the class the kind of place that they might visit and observe, e.g.:
- a local shop, supermarket or shopping mall;
- a bar or restaurant;
- a bookshop or library;
- a community centre or gymnasium;
- a cinema, theatre or concert hall;
- a dance class;
- a church, temple, synagogue or mosque;
- a public park;
- a local tourist attraction, e.g. a historic building or castle.

(3) In pairs or groups, the participants choose their preferred location and discuss the issues involved in this kind of visit, e.g.
- Will permission be required? If so, who from?
- How will the participants record their observations – in a notebook, or by using a smartphone, a camera or an audio recorder?

- Will the participants interview anyone? If so, what questions will they ask?

(4) The groups or pairs discuss in more detail the kinds of people and interactions they expect to observe in their chosen location. They might devise a 'schedule' to guide their observations or adapt the one suggested in Figure 7.2.

(5) Outside class, the groups or pairs then visit their chosen location with the schedule, describe the place and observe the behaviour and interactions that occur there, and take notes or recordings.

(6) In the next class session, each group or pair collates its observations, and devises a report on the findings to present to the rest of the class. In some cases, the teacher might suggest preparing an 'etiquette guide' based on the observations, e.g. recommended rules on how and how not to behave in certain public places, such as a library, cinema, church or park. Useful language for such a guide includes:
   - *In this situation, you can…*
   - *…is permitted*
   - *…is encouraged*
   - *…is expected*
   - *However, you are not allowed to…*
   - *You must never…*
   - *…is completely unacceptable!*

(7) In a following class, the pairs or groups present their findings to the class. Then, the participants share and discuss their findings with their online partners.

This is a generic example of a possible ethnographic activity with some language support. It will not, of course, be suitable for all online exchanges, but it is intended to suggest to organisers and instructors some of the ways in which participants' own cultural environment and experiences can be used as the input for practical ethnographic tasks that might be carried out by individuals or in groups. The basic format is adaptable for a range of online exchanges; the format is offered to readers here simply as a prompt for the design of tasks suitable for participants in their own telecollaborations.

## Participant Responses

Carrying out a more extensive intercultural activity than an ice-breaker requires participants to develop the kind of ethnographic and interpretive mindset favoured in intercultural learning. However, again, the online presentation of data, no matter how elaborate, should elicit responses from the participants.

An example of a participant response is given in Figure 7.3. This response, written by a European exchange student in Glasgow, was

> I dont think we get any street artists like this in Britain but I have definitely seen them when I have been on holiday in Austria, Spain and Malta and I think they are amazing as long as they don't suddenly move and scare you (That happened to me!)
>
> I will try and find my pictures!!
>
> In Britain people just tend to sing and play instruments on the street and they are generally not very good!!
>
> [Name] x

**Figure 7.3** Sample participant response

prompted by a detailed, written, online presentation about street performers in a public park in the Brazilian city of Curitiba. The presenter, a resident of the city, had posted an extensive study that included photographs of a human statue, a balloon sculptor and a flute player, alongside descriptions of them and accounts of interview data that he had collected. The online presentation was written in both English and Portuguese as a series of related posts.

The generalisation about the lack of street artists in Britain can, of course, be challenged. The responder was, no doubt, familiar with buskers in Glasgow but clearly had not been in Edinburgh at the time of the festival, when street performers such as human statues are normally very much in evidence. However, there are various indications in the response that the reader was engaged with the content of her Brazilian telecollaborator, to the extent that she was moved to recount her own encounters with such performers in Europe, and to search for her own photos of them to share. Her negative evaluation of the quality of the buskers she has encountered in Britain also offered the opportunity for further discussion, either affirmation or contradiction, among her peers in Glasgow. If participants themselves do not pick up on the possibilities for extending the discussion, it may be that the instructors decide to step in to elicit further posts on the topic. This aspect of intercultural learning is sometimes referred to as learning from 'rich points'.

## Learning from 'Rich Points'

One of the many roles assumed by instructors in managing an online exchange, mentioned by O'Dowd (2012: 355), is to guide participants in the analysis of any 'rich points' that emerge from the interactions. A 'rich point' (Agar, 1994: 99–101) occurs when ethnographic exploration reveals an issue that causes surprise, or consternation, and raises a question that demands to be answered. Rich points are unpredictable and emerge only once participants have observed and presented aspects of their own culture. Rich points might easily be overlooked by participants who have not yet learned to 'notice' effectively.

A rich point that emerges from the presentation of the Brazilian participant's study of street performers and the European participant's response is why the latter believes they do not exist in Britain, when they seem to be popular elsewhere in Europe. There are clues to the possible answers in the interaction itself: the European participant acknowledges that she has usually encountered such performers when she has been on holiday. There are clearly seasonal factors at work in some contexts that might be explored further. The European participant also remarks on the quality of those buskers that she has encountered in Britain, which raises the question of the training and background of the street performers: the Brazilian's interviews are revealing of the conditions of poverty and marginalisation that prompt some performers to adopt this mode of gaining remuneration. Participants might be asked if they consider such performances as a form of begging. The socioeconomic impulses that drive such performances in different countries – and the attitudes of spectators towards such performances – are 'rich points' that the teacher can raise for further investigation by participants.

## Conclusion

This chapter has focused on the design of intercultural tasks that go beyond the kind of 'ice-breaking' discussions that featured in Chapter 6. While an online intercultural exchange might focus on a series of ice-breakers and brief discussions in response to prompts, a more ambitious exchange will prompt participants to develop more extensive intercultural competences. Different ways of developing extensive tasks are possible but most encourage participants to develop an ethnographic mindset by observing their own culture, comparing it with that of their telecollaborators and discussing the 'rich points' that emerge. The organisers and instructors in a telecollaboration can design and negotiate a series of tasks that promote the development of an ethnographic turn of mind.

# 8 Negotiating Identity and Managing Rapport

Chapters 6 and 7 focused on starting interactions: prompting discussions and setting up more extensive tasks. This chapter focuses on those aspects of online communication that are required for participants to sustain effective interactions with others. In particular, it focuses on those aspects of *identity* that participants bring to the online intercultural exchange and develop during the exchange. The chapter also focuses on the kinds of language that are necessary for the establishment and maintenance of *rapport* between participants in an online exchange.

## Identity in Online Intercultural Exchanges

The issue of identity is a central one in intercultural language education; however, the question of how we should understand identity remains difficult to answer. The *Common European Framework of Reference* (*CEFR*; Council of Europe, 2001) guidelines offer a broad and flexible definition:

> As a social agent, each individual forms relationships with a widening cluster of overlapping social groups, which together define identity. In an intercultural approach, it is a central objective of language education to promote the favourable development of the learner's whole personality and sense of identity in response to the enriching experience of otherness in language and culture. (Council of Europe, 2001: 1)

From this perspective, 'identity' is defined and presumably changed by the network of overlapping social groups that any individual encounters. The optimistic objective of the 2001 *CEFR* guidelines was that by managing encounters with otherness, the individual's 'sense of identity' would be enriched. It is perhaps an indication of the difficulties of addressing this goal that the later *Companion* volume to the *CEFR* (North *et al.*, 2018) avoids any direct discussion of identity or selfhood. Indeed, the problems inherent in pinning down the concept of identity, as well as those inherent in static notions of 'culture' in online intercultural exchanges are discussed by Dervin (2013). Through his analysis of a case study, Dervin shows that exchanges do not simply reflect pre-existent identities, not even those aspects of identity that are conceived of in terms of apparently stable constructs, such as nationality, gender and faith. Rather, participants' identities are complex, fluid and dynamic, and thus are subject to redefinition and renegotiation within online exchanges. The practical lesson for organisers and instructors is therefore not to expect participants to display unproblematic identities in online exchanges. Instead of producing an 'enriched' sense of identity through the encounter with otherness, this very renegotiation of identity might well, at least initially, be a source of anxiety and tension among participants. One task facing instructors is to support participants who are undergoing processes that might be perceived by some as challenging or even undermining their sense of selfhood.

## Aspects of Identity in Online Exchanges

While allowing that all types of identity are fluid and subject to change, Anderson and Corbett (2015) follow Ushioda (2011), Richards (2006) and Zimmerman (1998) in suggesting that three aspects of identity are particularly pertinent to both language classrooms and online exchanges: *situated identity*, *discourse identity* and *transportable identities*.

An individual's situated identity is that which is conferred on the participant by the context; in the present case, it is the identity that the participant has by virtue of being a member of the online community. In Chapter 6, we noted that some participants will have a stronger sense of engagement with such a community than others. Online communities that are made up of voluntary participants who are actively interested in interacting with their peers will usually have a positive sense of their situated identity; other participants, whose membership of such a community is a course requirement, may have a less positive sense of their situated identity. As discussed in Chapter 6, one of the functions of ice-breaker activities is to strengthen participants' consciousness of their situated identity; that is, they should develop a greater sense of social cohesion with their peers in the online community.

Discourse identity is related to the communicative roles that participants play within the community. Online discussion groups again extend into the virtual domain those aspects of communicative behaviour that manifest themselves in the physical world: in any social group, some participants will tend to initiate conversations, some will be more inclined to respond and others will be largely content to listen. In online exchanges, members of the last category are sometimes referred to as 'lurkers' or 'vicarious learners' (Ridings *et al.*, 2006). There are numerous reasons why some participants might choose to 'lurk' rather than initiate or respond to posts; they may, for example, feel shy or they might simply be unengaged with the discussion topics. In this case, the instructor's role is to help build enough confidence and motivation for such participants to 'de-lurk' and move between the discourse identities of initiator, responder and observer as appropriate. The instructor, then, might have to monitor interactions, identify those who are lurking and encourage them to take more of an initiating or responding role. Alternatively, in telecollaborations that are assessed, participants may be awarded points for initiating and responding to posts. It is important to note that participants who largely confine themselves to 'lurking' might still be receiving some benefit from the interactions they are observing. The alternative label of 'vicarious learner' perhaps better captures the nature of 'lurking'. However, even if lurkers are indeed learning, one of the roles of the instructor is to encourage participants to assume a broad range of discourse identities, and so intervention in some cases will still be necessary.

The final aspect of identity is directly related to much of the content of online discussions: transportable identities. These are aspects of identity that are not specific to the context or related to the role in the interaction; rather, they are resources that can be 'transported' from one communicative event to another. Transportable identities include not only social constructs such as nationality, gender and faith, but also personal characteristics such as political allegiance; taste in food and drink; interest in particular forms of popular or high culture; pet ownership; love of sport as a participant or fan; and preference for certain types of hobby or leisure activity. These identities can be understood as resources because participants draw on them in the course of their interactions. Indeed, transportable identities are often displayed in the kinds of ice-breaking activities and discussions described in Chapter 6. If a participant identifies as a pet owner, for example, or as someone who is fond of animals, they might raise this as a topic for discussion. The interaction will invite fellow participants who also identify as pet owners or animal lovers, to share experiences that create stronger community bonds. The characteristics of the online community are co-created through interaction and the sharing of experiences by participants who identify themselves in particular ways. One point to note about the kinds of transportable identity raised in the early stages of an online exchange is that they tend to be – or at least usually attempt to be – non-controversial. Popular topics raised by participants in past exchanges include pets, favourite food or drinks, and lists (e.g. lists of favourite songs or films). These aspects of participants' transportable identities generally allow for group bonding without the risks of stereotyping or giving or taking offence. Once a degree of trust has been established, other, more controversial topics might be broached, depending on the circumstances and aims of the online exchange (see further, Chapter 10).

## Developing Rapport

For an online exchange to succeed, participants need to develop not just a community identity but what is widely known as *rapport*. That is, they need to develop a harmonious relationship whereby most or all of the participants in the online community are confident that they understand each other's intentions and feelings, and communicate their ideas well. To establish and maintain rapport, participants need to have at their command and be able to use emotional language, particularly indications of positive affect. As Anderson and Corbett (2015) observe, such indicators include:

- Attitudinal and emotional verbs, adverbs and adjectives ('I absolutely love this, it is great').
- Creative spelling to emphasise or intensify ('I am sooooo happy').
- Punctuation (especially CAPITALS and exclamations!!!).
- Emojis 😂.

Some of these features can be seen in the excerpt written by a local Scottish participant in an intercultural online exchange, in response to an icebreaking prompt by a fellow participant who sought to start a discussion about football (Anderson & Corbett, 2015: 191) (Figure 8.1).

Although there are no emojis in the excerpt, there are many other indicators of positive affect: the affirmative, opening 'YAY!!!!' in capitals with exclamation marks; the overt signalling of thanks with the participant's name mentioned; the emotional language, with intensifiers ('I absolutely LOVE', 'I do love', 'I am a fan', 'I am completely obsessed!'). There are also linguistic formulae that raise common ground between writer and readers ('you know'), and thus attempt to intensify the rapport between this participant and the rest of the online community.

A similar set of engagement markers (emotive language, exclamatory punctuation and capitalisation, etc.) is evident in a similar discussion opener by English participants based in Glasgow, celebrating 'fish and chips' as a stereotypical British meal. Two responses, both from Argentina, show different levels of rapport with the author of the original post (Figure 8.2).

---

YAY!!!!! I'm sooooooooo happy that a football (fitba) forum has been started. Thank you [*name*], you have made my year.

I absolutely LOVE football and have realised recently that I spend most of time talking about football. Although, recently it hasn't been too positive. I am a (Glasgow) Rangers fan... not just a fan... I am completely obsessed! I do love my team immensely but we are going through a really nasty spell at the moment which has caused a few tantrums, you know... kicking walls, punching floors, shouting, etc. and it has also caused some sleepless nights... I told you I am obsessed!

---

**Figure 8.1** Response to a post about football

---

**Response 1**

Hello You are right, I'm from Argentina and the only thing I know about 'fish 'n' chip shops' is that they are named very often in British novels. We don't have that kind of shops here.

**Response 2**

Hello! I'm [name] from Argentina. It's true that here in Argentina we don't have that kind of shop. However, we do have our equivalent here. If you ever happen to be in Argentina, more precisely in La Plata, you must try our special: 'milanesa con papas fritas'. Here in La Plata, young people go to what can be called a shop (generally in a square or park), where the special is prepared at any time. Generally, after going to a disco, like at 5am in the morning, we have 'breakfast' with one of this specials!!!!!!!!!!!!!

---

**Figure 8.2** Responses displaying different levels of rapport

While the author of Response 1 acknowledges the topic that those based in Glasgow had opened, and while she does offer some information about its cultural specificity as something she has only encountered in British novels, there is little explicit evidence of deeper engagement. There is a lack of emotive language, exclamatory punctuation, emojis and so on. The author of Response 2, however, seems to go out of her way to be engaged: while confirming the first respondent's information, she seeks to find an Argentinian equivalent to the British fish and chips, and offers *milanesa con papas fritas* as a candidate. The respondent explains how young people in La Plata consume this dish. The information combines direct address ('you must try this dish') with exclamation marks throughout the post.

Responses that display engagement to differing degrees, and thus build or fail to build rapport, can be used as the basis for in-class discussion – here, participants might be asked which of the two responses to the 'fish and chips' prompt might better encourage further discussion and why. Participants can then be asked to rate their own posts and responses in terms of engagement and likelihood of building rapport.

To a somewhat lesser extent, the linguistic features that display engagement and build rapport can be seen in a series of excerpts from contributions by four different participants to a discussion in a later telecollaboration about typical festivals in one's home culture, a topic initiated by one of the organisers (Figure 8.3). The generally lower sense of enthusiasm might be attributable to the fact that this is more of a class activity than an expression of a genuinely personal 'obsession' about something like a 'favourite dish', but the thread still shows the participants' attempts to generate rapport.

Again, most of the posts in Figure 8.3 develop rapport by displaying affect, e.g.:

I can say these are the *loveliest* occasion [sic]
I *like* to participate
I *really love*/I would *love* to visit/I *love* the fact
*really important* and *interesting*

---

**Participant 1: Israel**

The most interested celebration is Eid Elfiter and Eid Eladha because in this celebration, we go out with our families we visit each other and give money or gifts for children; we also buy new clothing for our children. Therefore, I can say these are the loveliest occasion that I like to participate in them. Related to others festivals there is nothing similar because this occasion relates just to Muslims.

**Participant 2: China**

It is very much like the most important festival in China: Spring Festival.

**Participant 3: China**

Hi there~

It's [name] here again. Among all Chinese festivals, I really love the Mid-autumn Festival, it is not the kind of grandest holiday like the Spring Festival, but it's still a really important and interesting one, both for families and individuals. Usually people would get together with there families on this day to have supper, moon cakes and watch the moon.(usually the moon gets to be almost the roundest on this day here in China, and 'round' can be translated into Chinese as the character '圆', and '圆' makes up the word '团圆' which means reunion, usually of families, so the round moon somehow indicates the reunion of families here hhh) Also, people may hang out and watch fascinating lanterns in gardens, on streets, I actually dressed in traditional Chinese suits and hung out with my roomates on the Mid-autumn Festival night this year, it was a lovely lovely experience.
I don't quite know if there is any festival in your hometown that would be similar to the Mid-autumn Festival, and I also wonder how is the moon like when it is autumn in the place you live.

The link below includes a TV show made for the Mid-autumn Festival, amazingly beautiful and creative, if you'd love to knows more about traditional Chinese culture, I think it would be a enjoyable option.

**Participant 4: Argentina**

Hi [name of Participant 3]! I would love to visit your country some day, chinese culture it's really intriguing for me, I know very little about your country but i've seen some films and documentaries and im really curious about your culture. I love the fact that there are so many celebrations in China, so many incredible (and very diferent from the ones of Argentina) foods, landscapes and music... i mean, China is on my bucket list, some day i would have enogh money to make that trip.
I wanted to tell you that there is kind of a similar celebration in South america, it's called Inti Raymi, it is the new year's for the Incas, it's still celebrated in Perú and some other andean regions. It happens when winter starts, at sunrise. They celebrate that the day after the solstice the sun will 'stay' longer, beggining a new cicle of the Sun, considered a God for the incas

**Participant 1: Israel**

Hi, [name of Participant 3].
it is so interesting to see how the moon is involved in so many festivals in different cultures because just like you, we Muslims also consider the moon to see when the festival will begin. I am extremely curious as to why the moon is so important in many cultures don't you think so?

**Figure 8.3** Responses to a prompt about festivals

it was *a lovely lovely experience*
*amazingly beautiful* and *creative*
*really intriguing/incredible*
*really/extremely curious*

Participant 3 is particularly effective at displaying emotion and attitude (at one point she indicates laughter: 'hhh'). Her post is much more extensive than that of Participant 2: she picks up on the comparison between Eid Alfitr and Chinese Spring Festival, adding details about the Chinese celebrations and also, crucially, expressing a personal element to them ('I actually dressed up...'). She also attempts to engage fellow participants in a prolonged discussion by explicitly inviting comparison ('I don't quite know if there is any festival in your hometown that would be similar to the Mid-autumn Festival, and I also wonder how is the moon like when it is autumn in the place you live'). She is successful in prompting responses from Participants 4 and 1, who focus on the importance of the sun and moon to celebrations in China, South America and the Middle East, respectively, thus identifying points of cultural similarity across the community.

The interactions of participants, then, can be used as the basis for classroom reflections on the expressive resources necessary to build rapport. Participants can learn from each other as well as from the instructor, noting useful expressions to try out in future interactions.

## Teaching Affective Responses

In-class reflection on the success, or otherwise, of responses is likely, then, to focus on the language of affect and engagement. As noted earlier, the differing degrees of rapport shown in responses such as those in Figure 8.2 can be used in in-class discussions. The organisers can ask participants in class to intensify the level of engagement in a less engaging post. For example, the response in Figure 8.4 is an example of a less effective participant response to the prompt that elicited the examples shown in Figure 8.3. The response shows little affect or engagement and indeed, on the evidence of the fluctuations in register and the varying degrees of linguistic accuracy, it might even be partly copied from a general description of Islamic holidays.

---

[Participant 5: Israel]

Hello everyone,
I would like to talk about Islam's Holidays.

First of all, it is important to mention that we only have two holidays in a year (Eid El Fitr & Eid El Adha). Eid El Fitr comes after Ramadan Month, we celebrate this 3 days holiday, we meet friends and family members and eat delicious foods...

And about Eid El Adha, it is 4 days holiday, It honors the willingness of Ibrahim (Abraham) to sacrifice his son Ismael as an act of obedience to God's command. Before Ibrahim could sacrifice his son, however, God provided a lamb to sacrifice instead. In commemoration of this intervention, animals are sacrificed ritually. One third of their meat is consumed by the family offering the sacrifice, while the rest is distributed to the poor and needy. Sweets and gifts are given, and extended family are typically visited and welcomed. The day is also sometimes called Big Eid or the Greater Eid

---

**Figure 8.4** Generic response to a prompt about festivals

Rather than dismissing such a response, instructors might use it as the basis for class discussion. The post is largely informative but lacks the personalisation and engagement indicators that might prompt a spontaneous response from fellow participants. The class can be asked to suggest types of information that would increase the level of personalisation and engagement, e.g. what 'favourite foods' does the author of the post specifically enjoy eating during the celebrations? Do people dress in particular clothes to meet friends and family? Is there a simple recipe for the sweets mentioned? How might the participant indicate more dramatically the enjoyment of eating the celebratory meals and sweets after the period of fasting that marks the month of Ramadan (e.g. 'It tastes SOOO good!!')?

A more challenging stance to take with respect to this post would be to invite its original author, in class, to consider what in the description of the Eid festivities might seem strange to those who are unfamiliar with the Islamic customs described. How might outsiders feel, for example, about the ritual sacrifice of animals as part of a celebration of faith and obedience? Are there festivals elsewhere that also involve the slaughter and consumption of animals? How might vegetarians celebrate this feast – or would that be impossible? The author might also be invited to consider whether any online partners belong to faith groups that also expect a period of abstention or fasting, e.g. the period of Lent for many Christians. Members of such groups can be asked if they, too, are aware of special meals associated with the breaking of the fast.

This stance is more challenging because it touches on potentially sensitive issues of faith and tradition that might conceivably cause the author discomfort if they are questioned or challenged. The instructors would need to exercise tact and judgement about whether or not to raise these issues, and (if they decide to do so) to raise them in such a way that the author of the original post does not feel that their beliefs are being threatened or attacked.

## Conclusion

There is, of course, no single set of universal linguistic features that will establish an appropriate level of rapport among participants in online exchanges across different cultures. Indeed, some of the markers of engagement used conventionally by some participants might be misinterpreted by others. For example, we have already mentioned that some participants from certain cultures will naturally end a post with one or more 'kiss' emojis, and thus apparently display a degree of intimacy that some fellow participants from other cultures might consider inappropriate. Depending on the participants' self-perception (e.g. their sense of their own identity as teenagers, young adults, mature professionals), there may well be differing degrees to which rapport is built through the overt display of emotional stance, and by the use of the language of affect and engagement markers. Not every online discussion group will be characterised by participants who like to display their emotions explicitly through the use of capitals, punctuation and emojis. However, for an online exchange to work well, rapport must somehow be generated among a group of strangers from different cultures, meeting in virtual space to engage in tasks and discussions in which they might have a greater or lesser personal interest. By analysing exemplars of posts that succeed or fail in generating lively threads, and by using the good exemplars as potential models, participants can develop a sensitivity towards those features that are likely to enhance the level of engagement readers feel when reading their posts, and develop their linguistic and cultural repertoires accordingly.

# 9 The Instructor's Roles: To Intervene or Not?

This chapter revisits the crucial role of the instructor in greater detail than it was treated in Chapter 7. Less experienced organisers of online exchanges might be forgiven for assuming that, once a partnership has been established and tasks have been agreed on, participants will interact and learn without much need for the assistance of instructors. Indeed, some of the authors of this volume recall having that naïve notion once. As O'Dowd (2012) has argued, however, the instructor, or teacher, remains a crucial factor in the success or otherwise of an online exchange:

> Studies have shown repeatedly that learners need the guidance and informed insight of their teachers to create their own online correspondence and to interpret and respond to the messages, blog posts and video recordings that they receive from their partners. It is in the classroom analysis of these authentic foreign texts that cultural 'rich points' emerge and the skills of intercultural interaction and ethnographic interviewing can be honed. (O'Dowd, 2012: 353)

A number of potential roles for instructors are identified in this quotation, from supporting participants in the composition of their posts (through classroom rehearsal) to the discussion of any 'rich points' that arise from the interaction, that is, as we noted earlier, the sensitive classroom analysis of what Agar (1994: 106) identifies as those issues that cause unease, invite reflection and so lead to valuable insights into cross-cultural differences.

Instructors are still necessary, then, but questions remain as to if, how and when they should intervene in intercultural exchanges in order to fulfil their crucial roles. There is no easy or uniform answer to these questions; reflective instructors will, in time, through trial and error, develop expertise that will guide their judgement. During the process of reflection, however, the concept of *scaffolding* might help to inform their developing awareness of how and when to intervene. This chapter reviews scaffolding as it relates to the instructors' roles in managing a telecollaboration.

## Scaffolding

'Scaffolding' is a familiar metaphor used, particularly, by educators who are influenced by the early-20th-century educational theorist, Lev Vygotsky (1934). The basic idea is simple: educators should provide learners with appropriate external support, or scaffolding, that will guide their performance. The guided or scaffolded performance will, in turn, lead to learners' internalisation of what good performance is. Gradually, the educators will dismantle the scaffolding, and learners will perform increasingly independently. There is, of course, more to scaffolding than this. For example, scaffolding should also give insecure learners the opportunity to build their confidence, before being pitched into a task that might otherwise be beyond their current abilities. However, an over-helpful teacher might actually hinder or frustrate those learners who are ready to act more independently, and so one of the qualities required of an experienced instructor in an online exchange is, simply, tact. That is, the expert instructor is one who knows when to intervene, to provide scaffolding, and when to allow learners to act independently.

Ribbe and Bezanilla (2013) present useful ideas about appropriate scaffolding for online learning. They identify the necessity for autonomous, 'proactive' behaviour by learners as a necessary prerequisite for online learning, and focus on scaffolding activities that should help develop this kind of behaviour. Following Little (2004), they identify three principles for effective learning in general, all of which can be applied to online exchanges: immersion into a learning community, learner involvement and learner reflection. Let us consider these in turn.

## Immersion into a learning community

The online exchange network functions as a learning community into which participants are 'immersed'. The network can have different layers, depending on the context and nature of the community. A participant might be part of a 'local' class or group that functions as a space for rehearsal and reflection, as well as being part of the more geographically dispersed online community. However, in some cases, the participant might be more isolated, connected only to the instructor and the wider network virtually. The instructor then has to decide, depending on the context, if and how to find space for rehearsal and reflection with the participants. If there is a local group, some face-to-face class time can be reserved for preparing the online tasks and discussing the responses. If the participant is more isolated, then the instructor might have to find time to do the preparation and discussion online, either individually or in a breakout group. Either way, the participants should gradually become immersed in the online community in which they will be expected to function so that they can learn from the experience. The instructor needs to support the experiential learning, possibly in ways that are suggested later in this chapter.

## Learner involvement

A second principle of scaffolding is that the learner be actively involved in the process of learning. This principle necessitates taking the views of the participants explicitly on board when negotiating the aims, content and expectations of the telecollaboration (see further, Chapter 4). Ideally, in lengthier exchanges, the direction of the exchange should be determined more by the participants' interests than those of the instructors or organisers. However, in the earlier stages, the organisers and instructors are likely to have a greater role in shaping the nature of the exchanges.

## Learner reflection

As we have also noted (Chapter 7), opportunities should be built into the design of tasks for participants to think again about their own contributions to any interactions, their responses and the threads in the exchange. They should be increasingly able to self-monitor, to evaluate their contributions and to identify and discuss 'rich points' that ensue from the interactions.

## Assessing Scaffolding Requirements

The most obvious way of assessing participants' scaffolding requirements at each stage is to ask them. However, participants may not be responsive to direct questioning of their comprehension or abilities, in part because they themselves might be unsure of what is required of the exchange and how their capabilities will match those requirements. Therefore, we can consider ways in which instructors might elicit participants' scaffolding needs at the three key stages identified by O'Dowd (2012) in the quotation that opened this chapter: the composition of posts, interaction and reflection.

## Composition of posts

Online exchanges may or may not afford opportunities for participants to rehearse their contributions in class or on a one-to-one basis with an instructor. If rehearsal opportunities are available, then the participant's class teacher and classmates can act as an audience for draft compositions. Process-based models of writing instruction (e.g. Susser, 1994) have long recommended an instructional cycle that can be illustrated by the following three steps:

(1) The teacher sets a task and the learners respond as well as they can to it; e.g. the task might be an ice-breaker or an ethnographic task, or the task might be to reply to posts made by partners in the online exchange. The learners respond with a draft of their own post or presentation.

(2) The teacher then reviews the drafts with the learners, and revisions and improvements might be suggested. At this point, the teacher might indicate generic models for certain kinds of posting (e.g. a post that elicits partners' views on a particular topic). These models should be considered possible resources for improvement rather than formulae to be strictly followed. The learners redraft.

(3) The redrafted versions are posted online for comment.

Process-based models of writing are good examples of scaffolding because in Step 1 the teacher checks the learners' current capabilities before seeking to extend those capabilities through revision and redrafting in Step 2. The teacher can therefore use the rehearsal phase to gauge the 'zone of proximal development', that is, to gauge the amount of scaffolding appropriate to the learners' needs, and then guide the learners to consolidate and extend their written competences.

## Interaction

If the compositional phase focuses on the scaffolding of linguistic strategies, the interactional phase, arguably, focuses on developing intercultural skills and attitudes. In a smooth exchange, information, attitudes and beliefs will be presented and discussed without friction, and without any need for the instructor's intervention. However, in some instances the very presentation of information about different cultures, and their associated attitudes and beliefs, will lead to participants questioning, offending or rejecting their partners. At other times, a misalignment of participants' understanding of the nature and workings of the exchange might lead to mutual exasperation or frustration. The instructor might then need to intervene.

One example of such a misalignment occurred early in an exchange between multinational European students based in a Scottish university, and a partner student in a Taiwanese university. In the middle of a lively ice-breaking discussion about 'favourite drinks, not including alcohol', the Taiwanese participant interrupted with a question that was clearly off-topic (Figure 9.1).

---

Hi, nice to meet you. May I ask you a question? What's your opinion about the transformation of women's status in your society in the past and in the present, in the west and in the east? Thank you for your help!

---

**Figure 9.1**  Off-topic response to a discussion thread

Out of context, the post shown in Figure 9.1 is perfectly well formed, if rather too wide-ranging in its scope. However, in the context of a spirited discussion of favourite non-alcoholic drinks, the post was considered to be inappropriate and – tellingly – insincere. One Scotland-based participant complained to the local instructor that the Taiwanese participant was simply using the group to find an answer to an essay question.

At this point, the interaction was on the point of breaking down. However, the local instructor calmed the group in Scotland, proposed a more generous interpretation of the Taiwanese participant's post and suggested drafting a response that elicited the participants views, as well as simply providing the requested information. The class agreed on a reply, which was composed by a German participant who was studying in Scotland (Figure 9.2).

The Taiwanese participant then responded in a friendly and appropriate manner and, after a few exchanges on the status of women, past and present, East and West, the thread returned to the original topic of favourite drinks.

The exchange is worth close examination. Drawing on the framework of conversational analysis, the diversion towards the status of women from the topic of favourite drinks can be considered a 'side sequence'. These are common in real-time, face-to-face conversations when participants become diverted and switch back and forth between topics. They are less commonly a feature of online discussion threads. In this case, the instructor had to intervene when one participant attempted to divert an agreed topic towards a quite different one, for reasons that were inferred as being self-serving. Her fellow members of the online exchange felt that she was departing from the tacitly agreed norms of interaction and wished to exclude her from the discussion. The instructor

---

Hi [name]

that's a very interesting but difficult question. I think, in most European countries, the status of women changed in terms of education. In former times, women were not allowed to study or have certain professions (e.g. teach at a university, etc); they were only seen as wives and mothers who had to take care of the household and the children. In German, we say that they were (and some men claim that they still are) responsible for the three 'Ks': Kinder, Kueche, Kirche (children, kitchen, church).

Fortunately, this perception has changed a lot and nowadays women can study whatever they want to and are considered equal to men (at least in most areas). There are still cliches and stereotypes (women cannot park a car, cannot repair or handle technical stuff, etc) but I think there will always be jokes and cliches concerning gender themes.

What is it like in your home country? Are you interested in any special aspects concerning the status of women?

Hope to hear from you soon,

cheers, [name]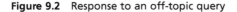

**Figure 9.2**  Response to an off-topic query

intervened to suggest an alternative form of action – one that actually enriched the exchange and that allowed the participant to remain in the online community and demonstrate the sincerity of her interest in the topic she had raised. The instructor in Scotland also contacted his Taiwanese counterpart and alerted her to the problems that would arise if members of her group continued to respond to posts with inappropriate requests for information. This prompted the instructor in Taiwan to discuss the need to post appropriate messages on the discussion threads, or to start new ones for new topics.

This example illustrates an intervention by an instructor to 'save' an interaction that threatened to lead to hostility towards one community member and potentially to destabilise the online exchange. There are also times when instructors might be tempted to contribute their own personal views to an exchange. Deciding how obvious and 'personal' an instructor's presence should be in exchanges requires some consideration, for the most effective degree of intervention depends on variable factors such as the sense of maturity and the participants' desire for autonomy. Teenagers, for example, might seek a more 'hands-on' approach from their teachers because they may be less used to initiating and maintaining online discussions in more formal contexts. More mature adults might demand a greater degree of independence from their instructors' views.

A crucial issue, which is bound to influence how frequently instructors intervene, is the extent to which participants actually welcome their weighing in. Regardless of their age, some participants may gain confidence from the scaffolding their instructors provide within the discussion threads, while others might feel that their instructors' comments detract from genuine interaction among participants. Those preferences are not necessarily made explicit by participants, and even if they are, participants' preferences might change over the course of an online exchange. Instructors should keep in mind that their presence and the overt expression of their own views on any topic might have the effect of encouraging participants to feel that the exchange is valid and worthwhile, and thus to make them more willing to speak up, but that it might, alternatively, make them feel constrained or self-conscious and therefore less disposed to take chances and to reach out to others. Of course, this is often equally true in physical classrooms. In both situations, instructors again need to develop a sense of tact, and not be too down-hearted if they make the occasional wrong call.

One important factor that instructors need to bear in mind is that their contribution in an online interaction is unlikely to be treated by participants as equal to theirs. In our experience, the expression of a point of view by an instructor can inadvertently have the effect of bringing a discussion to an abrupt end, as participants often feel that an authoritative response has been given to an issue. On another occasion, an instructor attempted to show the effectiveness of an ice-breaking opener that began 'I know it's a stupid question but...' (see Chapter 6) only to receive no responses to his discussion prompt. When he asked the local group why his prompt had been ignored, he was told, 'Teachers don't ask "stupid" questions'. It became clear that the members of the online community valued the sincerity of the involvement by both their instructors and their fellow participants, and that the intervention by this particular instructor was patently 'educational' in its agenda and insincere in its expression. Tasks that are perceived to be overly manipulative, and posts that betray a lack of sincere engagement on the part of the instructor or fellow participants tend to be ignored.

In short, for a variety of reasons there is no general or simple answer to the question of how interventionist instructors should be during online interactions. The most effective course of action is for instructors to elicit participants' preferences about their expected degree of involvement at the start of the course, and to try to monitor those preferences, directly or indirectly, as the exchange continues. One point about scaffolding is, naturally, that it should be removed – or restructured – over time, as the learners' capacities grow.

## Reflection

It is a melancholy fact, in our experience, that many participants in an intercultural exchange do not fully realise its value until it is nearing its end or over. To demonstrate the value of the exchange, it is useful for the instructors to set aside time for reflection, or as O'Dowd (2012) puts it, in the quotation above, to analyse the classroom exchanges thus far with a view to discovering and discussing 'rich points' that crystallise aspects of cultural difference and relativism, and so demonstrate that learning is taking place. Such reflection can follow ethnographic activities that focus on aspects of everyday life that might seem to the participants to be too 'ordinary' to warrant description and analysis. For example, one activity, 'Sofa Studies' (Figure 9.3), based on a task suggested in Corbett (2010), asks participants to describe and share activities associated with a common item of furniture, the sofa.

The activity might not, at first glance, seem likely to lead to particularly interesting insights. However, it is designed to elicit reflections

---

Describe your sofa in a couple of paragraphs. (If you do not have a sofa, describe the main piece of furniture in your living area.)

Choose an evening and keep a record of the main activities that people do on the sofa (for example, do they watch television, read, eat, drink or chat?).

How do people sit on the sofa? Do they sit upright, slouch, lie flat, sit with their legs tucked under them?

What does your sofa say about you and your family?

---

**Figure 9.3**   'Sofa Studies' (cf. Corbett, 2010: 58–60)

on aspects of everyday life. Two responses to this activity are shown in Figure 9.4.

It might not be immediately obvious to other participants in the online community what they should make of these posts or how they contribute to intercultural learning. At this point, instructor-led reflection might guide participants to look deeper than the comparison of furniture items and their uses, and to prompt them to consider how space in the home is organised in order to facilitate the relationship of individuals to the family grouping. The first response in Figure 9.4 is focused on the individual: the post tells of someone who (from the evidence in the post) seems to live alone, who has an office chair rather than a sofa and who relaxes in the chair by interacting with programmes and games on television. The second response describes a family situation: the participant's home has a small sofa that allows for communal television watching or socialising. The participant, however, also mentions a hammock on the balcony where she can read, study or relax privately.

Each response suggests possible ways in which individuals function with respect to a family group, or the lack of one. According to an influential model of intercultural communicative competence proposed by Byram (1997, 2021), part of *savoir être*, or 'knowing how to be' involves knowing how individuals relate to societal groups. By paying attention to how individuals and groups use space and furniture to organise themselves into familial groups with spaces for group or individual activities, the participants, in their developing role as virtual ethnographers, can develop a greater awareness of how individuals from different cultural backgrounds are similar or different in the ways they relate (or do not relate) to social groups in their domestic environments. The insights that arise from instructor-led discussion of these two posts can then inform the participants' reading of other posts on the topic.

The instructor may thus need to intervene to prompt and scaffold participants' reflections on the significance of the posts, particularly in

---

Response 1:

Hi, my name is [name], I'm in the Intermediate 1 group at Home Institute in La Plata, Argentina. we have been working on Sofa Studies. Actually I don't have a sofa, but I have a reclining office chair with wheels. I bought that chair because sometimes I work at home, but since the chair is very comfy I started to use it to watch TV, play videogames, watch movies and sometimes to travel across the living room (good bless the inventor of office chairs with wheels :p).

Response 2:

Hi! My name is [name]. I'm in intermediate English and whit my group it doing "sofa studies". My sofa it's quite small, it's for two bodies. it's so good for sit slouched, so i bought a hammock. It's there in the Balcony. i enjoy so much in the summer. the position it's so relaxing, and the balcony it's so comfortable when it's so hot. in my hammock, i study for the exams or read for my personal interest. my family uses it more the sofa, maybe for watch TV or only for be in the living whit some one more.

**Figure 9.4** Responses to 'Sofa Studies'

the earlier stages of an online exchange. Such interventions are partly to demonstrate to participants that they are actually learning. Once this has been done, later explorations of similar topics (e.g. the role of the kitchen table in communal meals or other family activities) might yield deeper insights from participants working more autonomously.

## Conclusion

This chapter has focused on the roles of the organisers and instructors in an online exchange. As noted at the start of the chapter, instructors' active interventions remain essential to the delivery of an effective exchange. Their contribution is not limited to the setting up of a community of online participants who share mutual goals and expectations; they are necessary mentors in encouraging participant involvement and reflection. They can do so by scaffolding the composition of participants' posts and responses, and monitoring and supporting effective interactions among them – particularly when those interactions may be in danger of going awry. Most importantly, though, instructors are needed to prompt participants to reflect on the significance of the posts they have exchanged, to look beyond the descriptions of everyday details to arrive at a more profound understanding of the cultural attitudes, beliefs and behaviours that underlie them.

# 10 Coping with Problems

Because online communities bring together learners from multiple localities and backgrounds, they afford their participants uniquely interesting opportunities to enhance their intercultural communicative competence in ways that we discussed in the previous chapters. However, they may also bring about challenges that even experienced organisers and instructors sometimes find difficult to overcome. Some of these issues are technical; telecollaborations are ultimately reliant on technology and technology can cause problems. Other issues are human. Regardless of how much we prepare, discuss and even intervene pre-emptively, things can go wrong. Sometimes by accident and sometimes as a result of intentional misconduct, participants might give or take offence, or become frustrated and upset. No matter how carefully organisers and instructors try to anticipate such problems, there will always be an element of unpredictability in telecollaborations. Nevertheless, devising and sharing strategies to respond to unforeseen, simple or complex obstacles is an essential part of the success of any intercultural initiative. This chapter discusses a number of the issues that instructors and organisers encounter and considers what can be done about them. The topics we address in turn are technical problems, sensitive interpersonal issues that might threaten the relationship among participants, and friction among instructors and organisers.

## Technical Issues

Chapter 3 covered issues to be considered when selecting an appropriate platform for a telecollaboration. A key factor in this selection is how familiar with the technology participants are and how user-friendly it is. The instructors and the participants in a project will inevitably display varying degrees of skill in their use of the chosen platform and have different degrees of mastery of its functionalities. One issue that can arise is that, once the platform has been chosen by organisers, some instructors and participants might express unease about their competence to use it effectively. It is a common assumption, suggested initially by Marc Prensky (2001), that relatively younger participants, whom he described as 'digital natives', born into a world in which instant global communication is taken for granted, will feel more at ease with the technology than many of their more mature instructors, who are 'digital immigrants'. This assumption has since been challenged; for example, Harmer (2013) argues that it is not age that is a factor in individuals' comfort with a given website or app, but the frequency of their use of it, and the quality of their engagements with it. Prince (2016), accordingly, has suggested replacing Prensky's distinction with one between 'digital residents' and 'digital tourists'.

To support the move from 'digital tourism' to 'digital residency', then, before the exchange begins, organisers need to be prepared to answer questions from their counterparts, instructors and participants about how text, images and files can be posted and responded to. Organisers of exchanges might identify one of their group who has sufficient competence and experience of using the technology, and who is willing to be approached for technical advice. Having a named 'tech guru' to contact on any project is a considerable asset.

Disruption of the platform itself is always a slight possibility, as even websites maintained by large companies are occasionally subject to technical failure and attacks from hackers. While major platforms tend to be well protected from such issues, the organisers of an intercultural exchange should still be prepared to deal with them. The most immediate step is to contact the platform's own support service, which might be enough to address most issues. However, long-term disruption could also happen, with loss of content, and that would require a much more drastic solution, such as shifting to an alternative platform. For such reasons it is advisable to nominate one of the organisers to keep a back-up record of the exchange as it develops, especially if the telecollaborators have opted for a relatively untried platform.

Most technical issues can usually be overcome with patience and goodwill. Before beginning a telecollaboration on a new platform, it is good practice for instructors to try out some 'mock' interactions on a trial exchange, to get a feel for the affordances and limitations of the platform. This also raises the confidence of the instructors before the participants are directly involved.

## Conflicts among Participants

In Chapter 5, we covered the importance of beginning telecollaborations by raising issues of 'netiquette' and stressing the importance of the virtual environment as a safe site where all participants should show mutual respect. However, it is in the nature of intercultural exchanges to explore values and unsettle the taken-for-granted notions of identity held by participants and, indeed, instructors. Therefore, in spite of all precautions, there may be instances of intentional or unintentional behaviour that is inconsiderate, or otherwise hurtful behaviour. It falls to the instructors to deal with potential or actual conflicts that might follow.

Sometimes, without even realising that they are being offensive, participants may react in a derogatory or insensitive manner to statements made by their partners about their habits or preferences. They may also draw on stereotypes and offer biased opinions on practices which are generally associated with certain regions of the world. One such episode took place in one of our exchanges when a teenage participant in Europe responded to an 11-year-old participant in Vietnam. An anonymised version of the start of the exchange is given in Table 10.1.

Although the exchange is clearly unfortunate, it is interesting. The second participant's response is couched not so much in racial terms (though this cannot be discounted) but in terms of conformity to social expectations. The point of criticism appears to be that the first player is an 'NPC', which is slang for 'non-player character'. Originating in the domain of interactive gaming, it refers more generally to someone who lacks critical thinking skills. Participant 2 thus constructs his persona as someone who mocks those who conform to social expectations, rebels against social and educational expectations and wishes to look cool ('fire'). It is possible that Participant 2 wished to be perceived as engaging in good-humoured banter. Some online communities will consist of participants with the maturity and resilience to regulate their own discussions, even when offence might be given and conflicts threaten. Participants with highly developed intercultural competence should have

**Table 10.1** Example of an offensive exchange (anonymised)

*Participant 1*

Hi everyone!

(1) My name is *[name]*. Please call me King. My nickname means the leader of a country.

(2) I'm eleven years old.

(3) I'm into playing soccer, playing chess, painting and listening to music.

(4) My favourite season is summer because I can go to my hometown and play with my cousin, grandparents and I can go to the beach for swimming.

(5) I like going to America because in America I can play and study with American people and I can have new friends on over the world.

Nice to meet you and looking forward to hearing from you.

*Participant 2*

Bro like who you think you are?

You look like an NPC and you want us to call you 'king' hahahaha 🙂

+ you said that you like going to America because you can study with american people, like bro you are a nerd 🤓 If I go to America Im not even gonna look at a book, Im gonna flirt girls and look for some sneakers to look fire the skills to mediate their own disputes. It seemed, however, unlikely that an 11-year-old child would have the maturity or skills to cope with this kind of response, and so the organisers of this exchange were compelled to intervene to defuse a potentially difficult situation. For effective intervention to occur, agreed strategies must be in place.

Instructors should be monitoring posts and so notice that a potential conflict is brewing. They may then intervene when they spot an issue that they feel demands their attention. Additionally, all participants should be aware that if they feel threatened or offended by posts, there is a reporting mechanism to which they can resort. Participants should know that they can alert an instructor who will respond to the complaint. In such cases, our strategy has been to consult the participants concerned in the interaction offline to discuss appropriate action. Sometimes, a reminder of the 'netiquette' conventions is all that is required for participants to be reassured. At other times, an offending post might be removed and, if necessary, written explanations and assurances sought from participants that the behaviour will not be repeated. In the case illustrated in Table 10.1, the instructors were observing the interactions. When the problematic response was spotted, it was removed and the local organisers spoke offline to each of the participants. The first participant accepted the apology offered by the instructor, and the second participant gave a verbal assurance not to repeat the behaviour and was not involved in further problematic posts.

While conflicts are challenging to deal with, they can be powerful learning opportunities, particularly if the participants are more mature, that is, in their mid-teens or older. Another concrete example illustrates the kinds of issues that can arise, and the outcomes of instructors' intervention. In another exchange that we organised, one participant responded to a self-description posted by another participant from the same school, criticising the choice of words and trying to raise their level of critical consciousness (Table 10.2). Unfortunately, the response raised a legitimate issue in an insensitive fashion. One participant described herself as 'white' which prompted her fellow participant to suggest 'light-skinned' as a less 'racial' epithet. The response may have been well intentioned, but the tone of the response seemed likely to give offence.

**Table 10.2** Example of a problematic exchange (anonymised)

*Participant 1*

I can describe myself as, 1- ambitious: Because I have a lot of future plans that I want to achieve, 2- emotional: because I can't control my feeling i cry so easily, 3- white: because i have a very white skin.

*Participant 2*

I've also noticed that you said that you are white, which could be really misleading, we can describe ourselves with 'white' in arabic, but in English it refers to the racial status, when someone says they're white it refers to them as in a white native American for example, so a better word would be is to say light-skinned instead.

When the interaction was noticed, the organisers again removed the response and immediately contacted the local instructor of both participants, who agreed with the decision and handled the matter privately with them from that point forward. The private, offline discussion with the participants was an opportunity to address not only the concerns of the respondent in raising the problems with the original post, but also in how legitimate concerns about potentially racist language might be raised in a more constructive fashion in a supportive online community. The potentially incendiary response became an opportunity to attend to the linguistic resources required for self-description and for reflection on ways of giving tactful criticism of the terms used in such descriptions.

A key aspect of how to deal with the kinds of issues raised in this section is to treat them, where possible, as teachable moments, that is, simply as issues that are located at the more 'sensitive' area of the spectrum of 'rich points'. In a traditional classroom, a teacher might pause if such an issue were raised, and take time to digress and discuss the issue with the learners present. Instructors in an online environment need to find a virtual equivalent for such discussions. Depending on the maturity and social cohesion of the community, they might choose to conduct the discussions online and 'on record'. This might afford the opportunity for a collective reflection on the issues, and reinforce the principles of courtesy, fairness and respect that are the basis of 'netiquette'. However, in other instances, instructors might choose to take such discussions 'off record' and negotiate solely with the participants directly concerned, off-line.

## Conflicts among Organisers and Instructors

A significant amount of the preparations we described in earlier chapters is aimed primarily at making sure that all those who take on the role of organisers and instructors of the exchange are working under the same assumptions and towards compatible goals. However, educators' priorities may change, reactions to what goes on among participants may vary and interpretations of how the exchange is moving along may lead to conflicting perceptions about how to proceed. Additionally, depending on the nature of the telecollaboration, the roles given to different people may seem unclear or discomfiting to them. When disagreements among the organisers and instructors arise, there should again be clarity about the steps that can be taken to address them.

Maintaining open and regular communication among organisers and instructors is one obvious means of reducing the potential for conflict. Email groups or chat groups set up on social media apps are useful for keeping in touch; and instructors are advised to commit to regular online meetings to discuss the progress of the telecollaboration.

As a collaborative activity, the coordination of the exchange depends on the contributions of organisers and instructors whose roles and responsibilities might change and sometimes overlap. Again, depending on the context of the telecollaboration, there may be organisers and instructors whose contribution is demanded by the institution, and whose personal enthusiasm for the project might be low. Many educators have heavy workloads and a telecollaboration might seem like an extra burden, at times, even to enthusiasts. Some organisers and instructors might feel that they are taking on disproportionately heavy responsibilities, compared to their partners.

There are, again, ways of mitigating potential conflicts that arise from these circumstances. During regular meetings, the schedule and the responsibility for implementing tasks can be agreed. The organisers need to ensure that there is space for all opinions and concerns to be raised so that all organisers and instructors are aware that their voice has value. More experienced organisers and instructors can be supportive and remember to praise the efforts of less experienced colleagues. More experienced organisers should also be flexible and open to innovations suggested by new instructors. The possibility of reputational 'rewards' can be explored, in the form of, say, a newsletter or blog posts for the institution, highlighting the successes of the telecollaboration.

Conflicts and disagreements, while challenging, can be pathways to developing richer expertise in the ways telecollaborations can work, and in how to handle interpersonal relationships. As organisers and instructors, we can approach each new telecollaboration as a way of enhancing our own intercultural communicative competences, in a spirit of goodwill, humility and generosity.

## Conclusion

A degree of unpredictability is inherent in most endeavours, and intercultural exchanges are no exception. There are innumerable ways in which things can go wrong, but preparation and efficient communication among organisers and instructors can help anticipate them and so mitigate their impact, at least to some extent. While organisers and instructors cannot anticipate all the issues that may arise, they should have an agreed set of procedures to follow when problems do emerge. For example, participants and instructors should have clear points of contact, they should be aware of how to raise concerns and they should be confident that any concerns will be taken seriously and in a timely manner. Particular care needs to be taken to ensure that children are protected.

Even in the most unexpected situations, few problems will be unsolvable if coordinators are in regular contact with each other and work together to find constructive ways forward. There will be cases when participants or even instructors ultimately prove unable or unwilling to address an issue adequately. The priority, then, will be to do what it takes to avoid compromising the ongoing exchange, even as lessons are being learned about the reliability of partners and participants, and the feasibility (or not) of working with them again on future telecollaborations.

# 11 Organising a Videoconference

So far in this guide, we have assumed that telecollaboration will take the form of asynchronous communication using a platform such as Google Classroom, Canvas, Facebook or even simple email. Asynchronous communication allows participants in a telecollaboration time for reflection, discussion and rehearsal before making what we hope will be a considered response. Synchronous exchanges are more demanding of participants, and so are ranked higher in the updated *Common European Framework of Reference (CEFR)* scales of achievement for online communication (North *et al.*, 2018; see further, Chapter 13). Asynchronous communication also allows for easy communication over several time zones. However, if it is practically feasible, there is considerable value in arranging at least one 'face-to-face', synchronous exchange among participants during a telecollaboration. This chapter focuses on the pros and cons of organising a videoconference, and suggests ways of formatting such an interaction. Setting up a videoconference entails all of the issues we cover in this guide in a nutshell. Organisers and instructors will again need to address practical issues, agree goals in advance, consider the possible format of such an exchange, anticipate the kinds of interaction that participants will engage in and conduct any 'debriefing' with peers and participants that may follow the videoconference.

## Practical Issues

The practical issues involved in setting up a 'real-time' videoconference are different from those involved in setting up an asynchronous online exchange. The platform is likely to be different: currently, Google Meet, Zoom, Skype and Voov (TenCent Meetings) are popular, but, again, attention needs to be paid as to which platforms function in different parts of the world, and whether participants have easy access to them, individually or in groups. Organisers and instructors are well advised to spend some time familiarising themselves with the functions of whichever platform is chosen, for example by running a few 'mock' sessions among themselves before the exchange begins. If individual participants do not have access to devices that will run the chosen software, then a physical location might need to be found where participants can meet and use computers or devices that are compatible with the software or that have the necessary licences.

Time zones are an obvious issue to be negotiated, particularly if participants are scattered across the globe. Early morning in regions of North and South America will be late evening of the same day in parts of Asia, and around midday in Europe. It is very unlikely that videoconferences can be held in class time for every group of participants, and so consent from participants may need to be obtained for a meeting outside normal class hours. In some cases, voluntary participation at a designated time outside class hours will mean that a number of participants who have clashing responsibilities or commitments will be unable to participate in the videoconference.

Issues of etiquette are also relevant to the implementation of a videoconference. Issues to be discussed beforehand would be whether or not participants are expected to have their cameras on during others' presentations or during any question-and-answer session. Depending on the nature of the tasks given, questions might or might not challenge the values and attitudes of other participants. Another practical issue, analogous to those raised in Chapter 10, is how to equip participants to deal calmly with questions that they might find offensive, hostile or inappropriate. Instructors can also explain their roles as monitors and moderators of online discussions.

## Agreeing Goals

Before embarking on a videoconference, organisers and instructors should consider the goals that are most likely to be achieved through this form of exchange. Drawing on the *CEFR*, the kinds of competences associated with synchronous telecollaborations include (cf. North *et al.*, 2018: 97):

- Making a presentation, using clear and precise language.
- Discussing the presentation in real time, adjusting language flexibly according to context and using appropriate emotional expressions, allusions and humour.
- Anticipating and dealing effectively with miscommunications, cultural differences and emotional reactions from the audience.
- Easily and quickly adapting register to suit different contexts in 'live' interactions.
- Engaging in discussion with numerous different participants, understanding their intentions and the cultural implications of their contributions.
- Participating effectively in complex, live, professional or academic discussions, giving and seeking clarification where necessary.
- Evaluating, paraphrasing, summarising and challenging (where appropriate) arguments in live, professional or academic discussions.

Of course, depending on the nature of the telecollaboration, some of the goals listed above may or may not be relevant; however, they illustrate some of the potential learning outcomes that videoconferences might usefully address. The organisers and instructors can then devise tasks that are designed to support participants in learning the skills required to achieve the relevant goals. Some of these tasks can be rehearsed offline before the videoconference.

## Tasks

The kinds of ice-breaking and intercultural tasks outlined in Chapters 6 and 7 can be adapted for synchronous interactions and, if circumstances permit, there can be a period of rehearsal in-class before the participants go 'live' in the videoconference. When devising tasks for the videoconference, organisers and instructors should, as before, consider the intended learning goals, any input, each step in the activities, possible settings and the roles of instructors and participants. In short, the following are the kinds of activities that might be included in a videoconference:

- Self and group introductions.
- A report on an earlier 'intercultural encounter' that might involve one or more other participants.
- Showing something 'typical' of the local culture, explaining it and answering questions.
- Presenting information about the participants' locality to others (e.g. presenting a local ethnographic study), and answering questions.
- Giving personal or group responses to an object (e.g. a book/song/ film) or a current topical issue, and discussing it with others.
- Presenting a project on a given topic, and answering questions.
- Participating in an online debate on a given topic.

Instructors and participants should be aware that their responses to their partners' presentations and contributions are as much if not more important than the presentations and contributions themselves (cf. Chapter 8). The skills of listening, eliciting and interviewing are highly valued aspects of intercultural communicative competence, and these skills, too, can be taught and rehearsed before the videoconference itself.

## Formats

In our experience, an ideal videoconference should last between 60 and 120 minutes, notwithstanding unforeseen events and technical problems. Based on observations of synchronous sessions, Aranha and Cavalari (2014) state that participants usually dedicate the first 15 minutes of interaction to checking the functioning of the equipment and their own appearance on camera, and to attempts to establish positive contact (including clarifications about the spelling of names, questions about the age of the interlocutor, positive appraisals of interlocutors' proficiency in a foreign language and search for similarities and differences in the study routine). Given this pattern, organisers can estimate how much of the remaining time should be devoted to other tasks.

The format of the platform chosen for the videoconference will impact on the kinds of setting, interaction and feedback that are possible among participants. For example, one participant or group of participants might be tasked with presenting a five minute description of somewhere in the locality, for example, a local market. The presenter or presenters might give a prepared talk to the whole community using images, perhaps on PowerPoint slides, to illustrate the content. If the platform has the affordances of Skype, Google Meet, Zoom or Voov/TenCent, then listeners might use the chat function to raise questions. These posts can be addressed in the question-and-answer session afterwards.

Zoom also has a useful 'annotate' function. A simple ice-breaker we used in an early synchronous session had participants use the 'annotate' function of Zoom to mark their respective hometowns on a map shown on screen. The activity allowed all those who were present to have a more 'visual' idea of how far-reaching the telecollaboration was and also gave everyone an opportunity to feel more comfortable with the platform by using one of its interactive resources.

As well as presenting or debating with the whole community, most video platforms allow instructors to group participants in 'breakout rooms' to discuss particular issues, have smaller group interactions to prepare content that can be fed back to the whole community. For large online communities, these breakout rooms afford the opportunity for particular participants to get to know each other better. In the breakout rooms, we have found that a particularly successful activity was to ask participants to present to others an object that was meaningful to them. Given the opportunity to choose something more or less personal to share, participants often discovered something they had in common with each other and clearly enjoyed themselves.

## Conclusion

Like the other components of a telecollaborative project, videoconferencing has a number of advantages and disadvantages. From an operational point of view, the challenges are considerable, especially when it comes to dealing with time zones. However, in terms of motivation, it can add significant value to the project. In addition, as Aranha and Leone (2017) show, with due regard to ethical considerations (regarding permission for the use of image and voice) and technical constraints (to do with the ease of recording the session), videoconferences constitute an enormously rich dataset that can be used in understanding online intercultural interactions and further research projects.

# 12 Learners' Language as Classroom Data

One of the great advantages of online intercultural exchanges is that organisers and instructors usually have a record – written and perhaps spoken – of participants' interactions and presentations. Most online intercultural exchanges involve learners of one or more of the languages used in the telecollaboration. In the exchanges that we have organised and in which we have participated, the medium of communication has been English. The interactions and presentations provide instructors with data that can then inform language teaching activities that aim to consolidate and extend the learners' communicative repertoire. This chapter focuses on the ways in which instructors can analyse the language data produced by participants and use that data in debriefing sessions to enhance their linguistic competence. The topics focus on issues of accuracy and appropriateness, and how language awareness or 'consciousness-raising' activities can become the basis of the debriefing session. We also look briefly at how text analysis software, or corpus linguistics, can be used to analyse participants' output.

## Accuracy and Appropriateness

Participants' language data can be analysed from a number of perspectives, most obviously in terms of its linguistic *accuracy* and *appropriateness*. While these factors can be considered separately, they are related: since many computer-mediated interactions are informal, spontaneous and dialogic, they often display some of the characteristics of spoken rather than written discourse. Spelling and punctuation conventions might be flexible and creative, while the grammar employed might be legitimately non-standard, when compared to more formal written genres. In short, in some online written contexts, it might not be appropriate to be completely accurate.

Nevertheless, the language instructor can learn much about the performance of the participants from their interactions, and this learning can be put to use in further classroom activities that focus on either linguistic form or communicative function. We suggest that instructors do not correct linguistic 'errors' in participants' contributions to online interactions immediately, but that they use them as the basis for later language awareness, or 'consciousness-raising' activities (cf. Willis, 1996). That is, the data can inform future reflective activities that attend explicitly to affective dimension of language, linguistic accuracy and communicative function.

The 'language awareness' and 'consciousness-raising' approaches to teaching and learning are not new. Wright and Bolitho (1993) published an article giving a general overview of the principles of the language-awareness approach, principles that still hold true. They advocate classroom discussions of language data as a valid form of teaching and learning practice on a number of grounds. Paying attention to language data through close reading and analysis encourages instructors and participants to reflect on their attitudes to issues such as correctness and normativity (e.g. 'What is acceptable in an online post?'). This reflection invites participants to expand their linguistic repertoires so that they have more than one way of achieving a communicative goal. Regular reflection on these topics encourages participants to develop the attitudes and habits necessary to become autonomous, attentive users and explorers of language. To develop these characteristics, instructors can draw on participant data from the exchange to address the following topics during a series of classroom debriefings that analyse selected posts or presentations (cf. Wright & Bolitho, 1993: 300):

(1) How does the writer convey his or her *attitude*?
(2) How does the writer attend to the *feelings* of the readers?
(3) Is the language (spelling, punctuation, formality, word choice) *appropriate* for the post/presentation?
(4) How does the linguistic *form* relate to the communicative *function*?
(5) What *discourse choices* does the writer make (e.g. choice of structure, choice of vocabulary, choice of style)?
(6) Is there *variation* or *translanguaging* between first language (L1) varieties and/or different languages? If so, why?
(7) What is the function of any *non-verbal material* used in the post (emojis, gifs, photos, links, etc.?)

Points 4 and 5 in the above list, which relate to form, function and discourse choices, are particularly relevant to the pedagogical movement that came to be known as 'consciousness-raising' (e.g. Ellis, 1991, 1993, 2008; Rutherford, 1987; Willis, 1996). While language awareness takes a broader view of different aspects of linguistic use, 'consciousness-raising' or 'C-R' activities focus specifically on recurring patterns of grammar, discourse and lexical choice. Willis (1996: 73–80) suggests a number of activities for this specific aspect of language awareness. Learners are generally invited to:

- identify recurring patterns of usage and language forms in the data they are attending to;
- sort language data into classes according to structural and semantic differences;
- make hypotheses/generalisations about language usage and test them against further data;
- compare and contrast patterns of usage in their L1 and the second language (L2);
- manipulate and rewrite language in ways that reveal underlying patterns of meaning and use;
- recall and reconstruct elements of a text in order to highlight significant features of it;
- learn how to use reference works (such as dictionaries and grammar books) to extend their linguistic repertoire.

The classroom analysis of contributions to online exchanges can draw on the activities suggested above to enhance participants' awareness of how language works and develop their linguistic resources. The following section looks at how such activities might inform the discussion of sample data that we have drawn from previous exchanges.

## The Debriefing Session

Not all telecollaborations will be hybrid; that is, it is not necessarily the case that groups of participants will meet in a local classroom setting as well as online. Debriefing sessions can therefore be conducted either as classroom discussions or as online meetings among sub-groups of participants. Whatever the setting, participants can be shown selected posts or presentations generated by recent tasks and invited to reflect on the language used in them in accordance with the questions raised in the preceding section. One way to do this is to annotate selected posts with questions for discussion.

The following posts are annotated with questions derived from the inventory of issues arising from the language awareness and consciousness-raising approaches. The posts are written in response to a prompt that invited students to share and describe their favourite film or television series (Figure 12.1). Selected Responses A–D are shown in Figures 12.2–12.5. The figures are followed by a commentary that suggests how instructors might work through language awareness and consciousness-raising activities with their students in a post-exchange debriefing.

This week's focus is on local movies and TV shows. Tell us all about your preferences!

- Do you watch local movies or TV shows?
- What makes them special for you?
- Please post a link to a clip/trailer for a film or TV show that you like (preferably with subtitles in English).

Don't forget to interact by replying to other posts as well!

**Figure 12.1** Prompt

Hi everyone

I am [*name*], actually I don't like to watch tv at all but I like to watch Turkish films and English ones in general.

There is a TV show that comes once a year in Ramadan, which called 'رامز قرش البحر' my family and i every year in Ramadan, we break our fast and then we set all together waiting this program.

Basically, this TV show receives every episode of a famous character and presents many games, tricks and adventures so that the artist feels afraid because of the adventure that the artist Ramez is doing. Ramez is a famous Egyptian figure in the Arab world because of his fun and exciting programs.

[*link*]

**Figure 12.2** Response A

Hi! I don't really like tv shows from my country (Argentina) i don't even watch tv at all, but, I love movies. I don't think my favorite movies are from here as I'm a big fan of italian classics but there's also a number of really good latin movies. Right now im thinking of two really lovely argentinian films.

Sidewalls is a film about two lonely people that 'are meant to be toghether' and because of the tumultuousness of the big city they can't cross with each other despite living in the same block. Architecture and urbanism are a big topic in this film. It also shows Buenos Aires as it is, and I like that

[*Link*]

Las acacias is a very beautiful film about a mother and his baby girl from northern Argentina that needs to reach the capital city (Buenos Aires) and has no money to make the journey, so, a truck driver gives them a lift. At first this man appears to by really grumpy, but as the hours go by he beggins to open and these two individuals create a bond.

[*Link*]

**Figure 12.3** Response B

Hi! I really like watching TV shows, both foreigners and nationals. One Brazilian TV show I watched recently was Cidade Invisível, or Invisible City. It is an original Netflix show, from 2021, that currently has one season, but the second one has already been recorded. It's story is about a cop that goes to investigate the death of his wife in a city in the interior of the country and ends up discovering that the mythological entities from the Brazilian folklore exist, like the boto-cor-de-rosa (the pink boto), the mermaid Iara, Saci-Pererê, Cuca and Curupira, and that they might have something to do with his wife's death. It is a very interesting show and I highly recommend you watching it. Here is the trailer in English: [*link*]

**Figure 12.4** Response C

> Hello there! I don't have any preferences between national TV shows or movies and foreign ones. I remember watching 'Coraline y la puerta secreta' ( better known as 'Coraline & the secret door').
>
> It was released in 2009 and even this year it stills being iconic.
>
> It caused horror in most of the children who watched this animated movie because it started being a girl who could go into a little door in her new house and could change realities. Her fake family had buttons instead of eyes, but everything was beautiful and they treated Coraline well.
>
> Then, things get complicated, Coraline's fake mom kidnaps Coraline's real family and tries to force her to put buttons in her eyes, luckily Coraline figures out the way to stop her and save her real family.
>
> Unlike most of the kids, I wasn't scared of the movie it was and stills are one of my favorites.
>
> LINK TO THE TRAILER ( don't forget to turn on the subtitles): [*Link*]

**Figure 12.5** Response D

One reason why online exchanges provide good data for language awareness and C-R activities is that the contributions are focused on similar tasks: the writers are all trying to say similar things. The instructor then usually has a range of means of expression that can be drawn upon in order to raise the participants' language awareness. Questions that can be raised about the responses shown in Figures 12.2–12.5 include:

• How do the writers convey their *attitude*?

Here, the writers are prompted to describe favourite films or television series. Explicit markers of attitude in Figures 12.2–12.5, sometimes corrected for accuracy, include:

I (don't) (really) like to
I (don't) (really) like -*ing*
I'm a big fan of
I highly recommend
I don't have any preferences between X and Y
It was and still is one of my favourites

The instructor can ask participants to identify expressions of attitude in the posts, correcting them if necessary and then supplementing them with other possible ways of expressing attitude, e.g. 'I've never/always had a liking for'. The group can discuss the appropriateness of these expressions in different contexts, for example, by contrasting the relative formality of 'I highly recommend' with the engaging informality of 'I'm a big fan of'.

• How does the writer attend to the *feelings* of the readers?

There are few explicit indications that the writers of these texts are taking the feelings of their readers into account. The importance of the language of affect is touched on in the discussion of rapport in Chapter 8. At most, here, the writers use evaluative adjectives to describe their favourite films and TV programmes in the expectation that similar evaluations will be evoked in their fellow participants. Thus, the films and programmes are described as *fun, exciting, lovely, beautiful, (very) interesting* and *iconic*.

The writer of Response D perhaps suggests indirectly that participants might, like most viewers, have been horrified by the movie he has chosen to describe, if they had watched it as children: 'It caused horror in most of the children who watched this animated movie... Unlike most of the kids, I wasn't scared of the movie'. In the debriefing, the instructor might encourage participants to consider if this might be rephrased somewhat to address others' feelings more directly, e.g. 'If you had watched this movie as a child, like most kids I knew, you might have been terrified by it. I was one of the exceptions!'.

The class discussion can focus on how the acknowledgement of readers' feelings in the posts (or the lack of such acknowledgement) impacts on readers' sense of engagement with the posts.

- Is the language (spelling, punctuation, formality, word choice) *appropriate* for the post/presentation?

There is a legitimate debate to be had with participants on the extent to which posts in an online intercultural exchange are required to be formal and linguistically accurate. This question might indeed be raised during the preparation stage before an exchange begins, when expectations about the nature of the exchange are discussed with participants (see Chapter 4). In the brief discussion here, it is assumed that participants have agreed that the discussions can be relatively informal and that particular modes of punctuation and adapted spellings are appropriate when they are used creatively to express affect. However, they are inappropriate if they cause confusion and incomprehension.

There are a number of examples of potential confusion in the responses, but the most problematic is the first, Response A. It is unclear from the response what the writer is trying to communicate about the programme. Some of the language choices that contribute to this lack of clarity are underlined:

> *Basically, this TV show <u>receives every episode of a famous character</u> and presents many games, tricks and adventures so that <u>the artist</u> feels afraid because of <u>the adventure that the artist Ramez is doing</u>. Ramez is a famous Egyptian figure in the Arab world because of his fun and exciting programs.*

Further investigation revealed that the author is referring to a series of television programmes by Ramez Mohamed Galal Ahmed Tawufik, an Egyptian entertainer who specialises in playing practical jokes on national and international celebrities. Sometimes, Ramez' pranking of prominent public figures has led him to be criticised by the Egyptian authorities. Once the background is known, the meaning that the writer is trying to convey becomes clearer. There are issues around sentence structure and word choice ('receives every episode', 'the artist', '[do] the adventure'). The instructor might elicit a clearer rewriting of the post, such as the following:

> *Basically, in each episode of this TV show, the presenter, Ramez, plays tricks on a famous character. Sometimes he is afraid that his pranks will get him into trouble. Ramez has become a famous Egyptian figure in the Arab world because his programmes are fun and exciting.*

This rewrite might not actually capture the intention of the author of Response A – it is not clear, for example, why Ramez is described as being 'afraid'. Even so, the rewrite provides clarity by offering an explanation that is lacking in the original post. It also untangles the relationship between 'character', 'artist' and 'Ramez'. The main point here is not to arrive at a single 'perfect' version of the original post but to look at how alternative versions, with different sequences of information, different levels of formality and different word and punctuation choices, impact on the reader's sense of clarity and engagement.

- How does the linguistic *form* relate to the communicative *function*?

The issues of linguistic form and communicative function relate most directly to consciousness-raising activities. Here, the instructor might attend to recurring patterns that some participants are not yet using correctly. Some participants are still having problems with tense and aspect, particularly in combination with adverbs or adverbial phrases. The adverbial phrases are italicised in the following extracts:

(a) my family and i *every year in Ramadan,* we break our fast
(b) *Right now* im thinking of two really lovely argentinian films.
(c) it *stills* being iconic
(d) it was and *stills* are one of my favorites
(e) the second one has *already* been recorded

Some of these adverbial phrases are correctly matched with tense and aspect; others are not. Learners can be asked to identify the patterns and match structure to meaning, e.g.

(a) *every year* [=habitual recurrence] present simple
(b) *right now* [=present moment] present continuous

(c)  *still* [=present fact] present simple
(d)  *still* [=present fact] present simple
(e)  *already* [=indeterminate past] present perfect

There are, of course, other issues with the examples, to do with repetition of subject ('my family and I...we' in topic + comment sentences), the form of the adverb ('still') and number agreement ('it was and still is...') and these need to be discussed too. However, a recurrent issue for many learners will be to match adverbial time references to appropriate tense and aspect choices.

Once the learners have matched the adverbs and adverb phrases to the appropriate form of the verb phrase, they can test their hypotheses against other examples, most easily, these days, by looking at corpus data, searching for the adverbs and noting the verb choices for each. They can then adjust their hypotheses according to their findings (e.g. does 'still' always indicate 'present fact'?).

Next, the participants can compare the patterns in English with their equivalents, if any, in the L1: do adverbs and verb choices pattern in the same ways or not? They might check what grammar books say about tense and aspect in English, and look at the examples given in dictionaries about how to use the adverbs. They can then rewrite and manipulate the text examples to demonstrate their understanding of the patterns, e.g. 'I *loved* this movie *when I first saw it*, it *has always been* one of my favourites and it *still moves* me to tears'. Finally, the instructor can ask participants to recall elements of the post by prompting them in such a way that they use the correct forms, e.g. 'Can you remember what Respondent A's family does every year after Ramadan?' or 'Does Respondent D still like *Coraline* after all these years?'.

The exploration of linguistic form and communicative function can be relatively extensive; the choice of patterns to focus on and the extent to which instructors go through the different possible stages of consciousness-raising will obviously vary from group to group. Some participants might regard such language-focused activities as reducing the enjoyment they gain from interacting spontaneously with their peers, while others might find them a useful supplement to their exchanges. The instructor will need to present them with some care, by indicating, for example, their value as a means of making participants' interactions more effective.

- What *discourse choices* does the writer make (e.g. choice of structure, choice of vocabulary, choice of style)?

As with other linguistic features of online exchanges, the participants' attitudes to discourse choices and appropriate vocabulary and style might differ. Responses A–D follow a clear generic pattern: an informal greeting is followed by a statement about viewing habits (it is interesting to note that this is frequently a disclaimer about watching films or television from one's own country), and then the participant describes a well-loved film or television programme. The informality of the greeting sets the tone of relative informality for the rest of the post: participants sometimes choose less formal vocabulary such as 'cop' rather than 'policeman', 'mom' rather than 'mother' and 'kids' alongside 'children'.

As we have mentioned earlier in this handbook, one feature that sometimes causes discomfort across groups from different backgrounds is the means of closing the post – many from South America end their posts with the word 'kisses' or an emoji signifying the same message. This is seen as less appropriate by, say, participants who grew up in the Arab world, where overt expressions of this kind of apparent intimacy are less likely to be displayed and possibly may be misread. The debriefing session is one forum where awareness of this kind of difference can be raised, and conventions adopted that are 'owned' by the online community as a whole.

Again, rewriting part or all of a post can be a good means of raising awareness of the interaction between discourse structure, vocabulary choice and style. The instructor can invite participants to write more or less formal versions of a post, by changing the greetings and leave-taking formulae (e.g. 'Good afternoon', 'With kind regards') and opting for more or less consistently formal vocabulary. Once again, after the different versions have been displayed for class discussion, their varying impact on readers can be discussed.

- Is there *variation* or *translanguaging* between L1 varieties and/or different languages? If so, why?

It is almost inevitable that in an intercultural online exchange, different languages and language varieties will be displayed. In Responses A–D above, the most obvious examples of translanguaging are evident in the titles of the programmes and films described. In some cases, the titles are not glossed in English, e.g. رامز قرش البحر and 'Las Acacias', while in others they are, for instance, 'Cidade Invisível, or Invisible City' and 'Coraline y la puerta secreta' (better known as 'Coraline & the secret door'). Respondent C also refers to the 'boto-cor-de-rosa' which is glossed less helpfully as 'the pink boto' [=porpoise].

In such cases, class discussion might focus on the value of giving the original titles with or without the English glosses. The original titles give a sense of authenticity to the description while the glosses (when they are present and accurate) help the readers understand their sense. It is interesting that Respondent D notes that the Spanish film is 'better known' by its English title; it is not evident from the post itself whether this claim is, in fact, true. However, it does suggest that Respondent D believes that the global fame of a Spanish movie has been facilitated by its international reception under an English title, and, as such, the claim indicates the attitude of Respondent D to English as an international medium of popular culture.

There are, of course, other reasons for the presence of translanguaging in online exchanges. The presence of other languages can be identified and their function and significance within a text can become topics of discussion.

- What is the function of any *non-verbal material* used in the post (emojis, gifs, photos, links, etc?)

Chapter 8 discussed the role of emojis and other non-verbal elements of a text, such as punctuation and non-standard spelling, in establishing rapport between participants. 'Emojis', as their name suggests, are a means of explicitly displaying the writer's emotions, whether sincere or affected. There are other roles for non-verbal elements in a text. Photos, for example, are a powerful way of demonstrating aspects of the writer's immediate material culture: participants in an exchange can send images of their surroundings, their favourite dishes and so on.

In Responses A–D above, hyperlinks are given to third-party video material on another platform, such as YouTube or Vimeo. At the time of writing, not all participants globally have easy or unrestricted access to such platforms; the participants based in China, for example, had restricted or no access to YouTube videos, while their Western co-participants had little experience of using Chinese platforms such as bilibili. Restrictions notwithstanding, where participants do have access to common social media platforms, sharing video clips is another powerful way of engaging others in one's own culture and building a group ethos.

The writers above have attempted in their posts to frame the readers' experience of the videos in different ways. Respondent A invites readers to imagine themselves as part of a family, breaking fast after Ramadan and watching the programme as a social unit. Respondent B summarises each film, noting that 'architecture and urbanism' are 'a big topic' in the first, which, it is claimed, shows Buenos Aires 'as it is'. Respondent C observes that a global Netflix series is indebted to characters rooted in local Brazilian folk mythology, and 'highly recommends' the programme as 'interesting'. Respondent D recalls the traumatic impact that an 'iconic' fantasy film had on children of her generation, and acknowledges its lasting impact. Both Respondents C and D observe that the video clip is available in English or with English subtitles.

Each writer, then, invites co-participants to imaginatively share not just the video clip but the personal experience it prompts, which may afford insights into family life, city life, national legends or common childhood fears. As has been noted earlier in this volume, one challenge for readers is to take advantage of these insights and respond with corresponding accounts of similar cultural experiences.

## Building a Corpus of Exchange Data

Organisers and instructors who are blessed with sufficient time and expertise might wish to collect the contributions to an online intercultural exchange in order to build a digital corpus of interactions between participants. The corpus can then be easily searched for insights into language that might escape the analysis of individual posts or a small sample of posts, such as in Figures 12.2–12.5. One relatively simple way of doing this is to compile the texts and analyse them with a text analysis program such as AntConc (Anthony, 2021) or WordSmith (Scott, 2020).

The analysis of a digital corpus of online intercultural exchanges can be guided by the language awareness and consciousness-raising framework illustrated in the preceding section. Over seven years, Wendy Anderson (Anderson & Corbett, 2015) built a small corpus (c. 29,000 words) of participant-initiated contributions to online intercultural exchanges that included native and non-native speakers. She used this small corpus to study the language of affect in participant-initiated ice-breakers; that is, in terms of language awareness, she explored the language of feelings, specifically evaluations. Anderson found that positive adjectives outnumbered negative ones, both in range and frequency of use, and that there was a general disinclination to use explicitly negative adjectives in online exchanges. In other words, participants preferred to say that something was 'not nice' rather than 'nasty'. The most frequently used verbs of appraisal were 'love' and 'like' and a sample set of concordance lines shows how they were used:

| (1) | the thing I would | **like** | to do for the rest of my life |
|---|---|---|---|
| (2) | I also | **like** | dancing |
| (3) | I really don't | **like,** | actually I hate it |
| (4) | I do | **like** | cats, but… |
| (5) | we would | **like** | to share our bucket list |
| (6) | and generally I | **love** | animals. Once |
| (7) | I | **love** | shopping! However |
| (8) | hard ones and I | **love** | it when the bottom goes all squishy |
| (9) | with dolphins…I would really | **love** | to do it! |
| (10) | I really | **love** | to visit quite different places |

The sample concordance lines illustrate the most frequent uses of 'like' and 'love' with a first-person subject. Anderson and Corbett (2015: 187–188) observe relatively few third-person subjects or elicitations ('Do you like…?'), coming to the conclusion that such posts are generally seen by participants as an opportunity and space to express positive appraisals about aspects of their transportable identities (cf. Chapter 8, this volume).

Text analysis of even a modest, bespoke corpus of interactions, then, can indicate patterns that are not verifiable by analysis of individual posts or small groups of posts. Another use of an online corpus of non-native speaker interactions is simply as a corpus of learner English. This can identify patterns of inappropriate or incorrect usage that can be used to inform later consciousness-raising activities, e.g. what structures normally follow 'recommend', as in Respondent D's 'I highly recommend you watching it'? The patterns in the learner corpus can be compared with patterns in a reference corpus of standard English.

## Conclusion

Not all organisers of online intercultural exchanges will wish to integrate the exchange with the analysis of language data for further learning. Some may decide that the exchange itself is a worthwhile activity for the development of aspects of intercultural competence. For those who do wish to explicitly combine intercultural competence with the development of a broader communicative repertoire, however, the data generated by online intercultural exchanges represents an extremely rich resource that can inform language awareness and consciousness-raising activities. Online exchanges prompt different posts that are focused on comparable rhetorical action; in other words, different people attend to the same task, using different language to achieve similar goals. Their linguistic choices become the substance of language awareness and C-R discussions. The procedures illustrated in this chapter can be transferred to different sets of data, e.g. various samples from the threads generated by a prompt. Given sufficient time and energy, organisers might also consider gradually, building a corpus of exchanges and using that to extend the kinds of exploration of linguistic form and communicative function favoured by advocates of language awareness and consciousness-raising. With a broader communicative repertoire, participants should be able to engage more effectively in online intercultural exchanges.

# 13 Assessing Participants' Performance

This chapter deals with the assessment of participants' contributions to an online intercultural exchange. This is distinct from the evaluation of the course itself, which will be the topic of Chapter 14. This chapter deals with possible ways of assessing participants' posts and responses as part of a language learning programme or as part of a teacher education programme. We cannot anticipate all of the many contexts in which online exchanges occur and the purposes that they might have: online exchanges might be voluntary, extra-curricular activities that might not need to be formally assessed, or they might be arranged with a particular set of intended learning outcomes with respect to language and culture. Some course organisers might set up a particular online exchange to explore participants' developing understanding of certain aspects of culture, e.g. their attitudes to current affairs reporting, gender roles in different communities, their different experiences of education and schooling, their awareness of the impact of tourism on local communities or perspectives on the etiquette and protocols to be followed in business negotiations across cultures.

One advantage of the formal assessment of online intercultural exchanges – even if it is not required by the institution or organisers – is that it gives participants a sense of achievement and learning by the end of the project. Assessment can raise participants' levels of awareness of what is at stake, linguistically and culturally, in an online exchange. In short, assessment promotes reflection. It is therefore worthwhile for organisers at least to consider incorporating into their exchange some explicit assessment that promotes reflection on the learning that has occurred. This chapter offers guidance in using assessment instruments to foster participants' learning. We consider the general advantages and disadvantages of using the *Common European Framework of Reference (CEFR)*, before looking more closely at particular *CEFR* assessment scales that are most obviously relevant to telecollaboration. We argue that these scales can be modified by organisers and instructors to meet the need to assess participants' contributions to their own exchanges.

## The *Common European Framework of Reference*

While there are many potential approaches to assessing the learning of language and culture, the one that we adopt in this brief guide draws on the expertise of those educators who designed the scales of achievement that form the basis of the *CEFR* (Council of Europe, 2001; North *et al.*, 2018). There are advantages and disadvantages to using the *CEFR*. On the plus side, it is a widely known set of assessment criteria that provides a common benchmark for countries both within and beyond the continent of Europe (Byram & Parmenter, 2012). Furthermore, from the outset, the *CEFR* was designed as a framework that would incorporate intercultural competence alongside linguistic competences (Council of Europe, 2001: 1). The *Companion* volume (North *et al.*, 2018) updates the extensive guidelines of the original framework, and usefully refocuses it towards mediation. 'Mediation' in the *Companion* is a complex concept, at times referring to the ways in which conceptual categories are aligned with a particular worldview, at times referring to the search for linguistic and conceptual equivalences across cultures, and at times referring to strategies to mitigate misunderstanding and conflict when concepts are misaligned or exact equivalences are lacking (Corbett, 2021).

Online intercultural exchanges, then, can be understood as potential sites in which participants might mediate aspects of their own culture to enhance empathic understanding between themselves and others. The process of mediation is realised by the posts and responses, and by the presentations and discussion threads prompted by the tasks. These texts are occasions for the expression of a worldview, the comparison of worldviews and the discussion of similarities and differences. Assessment focuses on participants' demonstration that they are in possession of a linguistic repertoire for expressing, comparing and discussing their worldviews, and that they possess the intercultural competences necessary to complete given tasks. The assessment needs also to take into consideration the fact that many of the activities are conducted online, though there may be in-class preparation, rehearsal and post-exchange reflection that can also be made subject to assessment.

The advantage of the *CEFR*, in short, is that it provides a widely recognised and relevant framework for assessment purposes. On the negative side, it has been criticised on a number of grounds. For example, some of the contributions to Byram and Parmenter (2012) question the wider relevance of a European document that is intended primarily to promote plurilingualism and a set of common values among a particular group of nations. Although used far beyond Europe, the *CEFR* can be seen as a values-based social intervention intended primarily to promote harmony among the linguistically and culturally diverse nations of Europe, a goal that is not necessarily applicable elsewhere.

Secondly, the *CEFR*'s approach to assessing interculturality is to 'atomise' aspects of intercultural communicative competence into discrete skills and attitudes; some intercultural educators take exception to the dismemberment of what they see as a fundamentally holistic quality that should be assessed, if at all, in a holistic fashion (cf. Liddicoat & Scarino, 2020: 403). That said, the original *CEFR* acknowledged the limitations of this aspect of its approach to assessment, noting that while its assessment instruments focused on different, overlapping aspects of intercultural communicative competence, its authors' assumption was that, when combined, they would act as an index of overall achievement (Council of Europe, 2001: 1).

A final argument in favour of using scales of achievement drawn from the *CEFR* is that these instruments of assessment have been shown to be consistently and reliably applicable by non-expert raters (Fulcher, 2015: 79). While bearing in mind critiques of the *CEFR* and similar universalising sets of assessment criteria, there still seems to be an educational value in developing scales of achievement based on the *CEFR* in order to harmonise assessment across the locations in which telecollaboration takes place.

The following sections consider three of the *CEFR* scales of achievement from the 2018 *Companion* that seem particularly relevant to online intercultural exchanges. Two scales of achievement in the revised *Companion* specifically address online interaction and telecollaboration; a further, more general, set of scales on mediation is also discussed below.

## *CEFR* Guidelines for Online Conversation and Discussion

The scales of achievement for online conversation and discussion are presented in North *et al.* (2018: 96–98) and Table 13.1 reproduces the scales of achievement related to this aspect of competence (North *et al.*, 2018: 97). The relevance of this scale is limited in its potential application to online intercultural exchanges in that progression up the scale assumes a move from asynchronous to synchronous communicative events (which are considered to be more challenging), and from less formal discussions to more formal communicative events, such as business meetings and academic seminars. This progression from asynchronous to synchronous might not apply to every online exchange (although some exchanges may incorporate synchronous events; see Chapter 11) and not every online exchange will progress from informal discussion to formal presentation or seminar (though, as Chapter 7 explains, different kinds of tasks can be designed that may include opportunities to display different linguistic repertoires and skills).

Even so, the *CEFR* scale of achievement remains useful in helping organisers and instructors to clarify what they might wish to assess in

**Table 13.1**    *CEFR* scales of achievement for online conversation and discussion

| Online conversation and discussion |
|---|
| **C2** Can express him/herself with clarity and precision in real-time online discussion, adjusting language flexibly and sensitively to context, including emotional, allusive and joking usage.<br><br>Can anticipate and deal effectively with possible misunderstandings (including cultural ones), communication issues and emotional reactions occurring in an online discussion.<br><br>Can easily and quickly adapt his/her register and style to suit different online environments, communication purposes and speech acts. |
| **C1** Can engage in real-time online exchanges with several participants, understanding the communicative intentions and cultural implications of the various contributions.<br><br>Can participate effectively in live, online professional or academic discussion, asking for and giving further clarification of complex, abstract issues as necessary.<br><br>Can adapt his/her register according to the context of an online interaction, moving from one register to the other within the same exchange if necessary.<br><br>Can evaluate, restate and challenge arguments in professional or academic live online chat and discussion. |
| **B2** Can engage in online exchanges, linking his/her contributions to previous ones in the thread, understanding cultural implications and reacting appropriately.<br><br>Can participate actively in an online discussion, stating and responding to opinions on topics of interest at some length, provided contributors avoid unusual or complex language and allow time for responses.<br><br>Can engage in online exchanges between several participants, effectively linking his/her contributions to previous ones in the thread, provided a moderator helps manage the discussion.<br><br>Can recognise misunderstandings and disagreements that arise in an online interaction and can deal with them, provided that the interlocutor(s) is willing to cooperate. |
| **B1** Can engage in real-time online exchanges with more than one participant, recognising the communicative intentions of each contributor, but may not understand details or implications without further explanation.<br><br>Can post online accounts of social events, experiences and activities referring to embedded links and media and sharing personal feelings.<br><br>Can post a comprehensible contribution in an online discussion on a familiar topic of interest, provided that he/she can prepare the text beforehand and use online tools to fill gaps in language and check accuracy.<br><br>Can make personal online postings about experiences, feelings and events and respond individually to the comments of others in some detail, though lexical limitations sometimes cause repetition and inappropriate formulation. |
| **A2** Can introduce him/herself and manage simple exchanges online, asking and answering questions and exchanging ideas on predictable everyday topics, provided enough time is allowed to formulate responses, and that he/she interacts with one interlocutor at a time.<br><br>Can make short descriptive online postings about everyday matters, social activities and feelings, with simple key details.<br><br>Can comment on other people's online postings, provided that they are written in simple language, reacting to embedded media by expressing feelings of surprise, interest and indifference in a simple way.<br><br>Can engage in basic social communication online (e.g. writing a simple message on a virtual card for a special occasion, sharing news and making/confirming arrangements to meet).<br><br>Can make brief positive or negative comments online about embedded links and media using a repertoire of basic language, though he/she will generally have to refer to an online translation tool and other resources. |

*(Continued)*

**Table 13.1**   (Continued)

| Online conversation and discussion |
| --- |

| | |
| --- | --- |
| A1 | Can write very simple messages and personal online postings as a series of very short sentences about hobbies, likes/dislikes, etc., relying on the aid of a translation tool.
Can use formulaic expressions and combinations of simple words to post short positive and negative reactions to simple online postings and their embedded links and media, and can respond to further comments with standard expressions of thanks and apology. |
| Pre-A1 | Can post simple online greetings, using basic formulaic expressions and emoticons.
Can post online short simple statements about him/herself (e.g. relationship status, nationality, occupation), provided he/she can select them from a menu and/or refer to an online translation tool. |

Source: North *et al.* (2018: 97).

terms of language and intercultural competence in basic online interactions. The design of this scale of achievement takes into consideration, among other things, the importance of participants' 'ability to handle emotional reactions' (cf. Chapter 8 in the present volume) and the authors claim that it operationalises certain 'key concepts' that include the following (North *et al.*, 2018: 96):

- composing posts and contributions for others to respond to;
- comments (e.g. evaluative) on posts, comments and contributions of others;
- reactions to embedded media;
- the ability to include symbols, images and other codes for making the message convey tone;
- stress and prosody, but also the affective/emotional side, irony, etc.

The key concepts to be assessed in this scale of achievement involve aspects of the participants' discourse identities discussed in Chapter 8: are they 'initiators, responders or lurkers', and how well do they manage rapport in their posts, by means such as evaluation, affective language, punctuation, creative spelling and non-verbal symbols such as emojis?

The interactional and affective aspects of an asynchronous online intercultural exchange can be extracted from the lower regions of the scale of achievement reproduced in Table 13.1, and elements from the higher categories (B2–C1) can also be adapted if there is a synchronous component in the online intercultural exchange. For example, if the exchange involves more mature university students, their interactions might progress towards a shared event – possibly a videoconference – in the form of an academic seminar, and so the exchange might involve the kind of language repertoire suitable for assessment at the C1 or even C2 level. Otherwise, an alternative scale of achievement might be used. North *et al.* (2018: 98–99) offer a scale specifically designed to assess online collaborative and transactional tasks.

Like the scale of achievement reproduced in Table 13.1, the assessment instrument in the *CEFR Companion* that relates to goal-oriented online collaborations and transactions is not designed specifically for online *intercultural* exchanges, but it can be adapted for use by exchange organisers and instructors. The key concepts addressed by this set of descriptors are as follows (North *et al.*, 2018: 98):

- purchasing goods and services online;
- engaging in transactions requiring negotiation of conditions, in a service as well as client role;
- participating in collaborative project work;
- dealing with communication problems.

The scale thus combines two different scenarios that share an orientation towards a goal: accomplishing an online transaction (such as ordering some product online) and collaborating to achieve some kind of shared task. It is the latter scenario that is more obviously applicable to intercultural telecollaborations in which participants are invited to work together to produce, say, a presentation on a topic of shared interest, such as a guide to tourist sites in their respective locations. Table 13.2 shows an adapted version of the scale of achievement suggested in the *Companion*, with a focus solely on the collaborative element. This time the progression from A1 to C2 is not dependent on participants extending their repertoire into different types of communicative event, but 'the move towards higher levels expands from basic transactions and information exchange at the A levels towards more sophisticated collaborative project work that is goal-oriented' at the C levels (North *et al.*, 2018: 98).

Instructors and organisers can develop tasks of different types that may be assessed using scales such as those suggested in Table 13.2. For some tasks set during an online exchange, more linguistically proficient partners might be paired with less proficient partners. For example, participants at the B2–C1 level might be required to interview one or more participants at the A1–B1 level on a topic such as their engagement with popular culture (e.g. television, music, social media). The more advanced participants can work in collaboration to produce an online survey or questionnaire that the less advanced participants answer. In general, assessment tasks should demonstrate the participants' competences at their assumed level of proficiency and they should offer participants an opportunity to demonstrate the range of their linguistic repertoire and intercultural competences.

In short, the achievement scales shown in Tables 13.1 and 13.2 can be adapted and employed by exchange organisers and instructors for the assessment of a diversity of task types to be accomplished online by participants across different localities.

**Table 13.2**   *CEFR* scales of achievement for online goal-oriented collaboration

| Online goal-oriented collaboration | |
| --- | --- |
| C2 | Can resolve misunderstandings and deal effectively with frictions that arise during the collaborative process. |
| | Can provide guidance and add precision to the work of a group at the redrafting and editing stages of collaborative work. |
| C1 | Can coordinate a group who are working on a project online, formulating and revising detailed instructions, evaluating proposals from team members and providing clarifications in order to accomplish the shared tasks. |
| | Can participate in complex projects requiring collaborative writing and redrafting as well as other forms of online collaboration, following and relaying instructions with precision in order to reach the goal. |
| | Can deal effectively with communication problems and cultural issues that arise in an online collaborative exchange by reformulating, clarifying and exemplifying through media (visual, audio, graphic). |
| B2 | Can take a lead role in online collaborative work within his/her area(s) of expertise, keeping the group on task by reminding them of roles, responsibilities and deadlines in order to achieve established goals. |
| | Can engage in online collaborative exchanges within his/her area(s) of expertise that require negotiation and explanation of complicated details and special requirements. |
| | Can deal with misunderstandings and unexpected problems that arise in online collaborative exchanges by responding politely and appropriately in order to help resolve the issue. |
| | Can collaborate online with a group that is working on a project, justifying proposals, seeking clarification and playing a supportive role in order to accomplish shared tasks. |
| B1 | Can interact online with a group that is working on a project, following straightforward instructions, seeking clarification and helping to accomplish the shared tasks. |
| | Can engage in online collaborative exchanges that require simple clarification or an explanation of relevant details, such as registering for a course, tour, event or applying for membership. |
| | Can interact online with a partner or small group working on a project, provided there are visual aids such as images, statistics and graphs to clarify more complex concepts. |
| | Can respond to instructions and ask questions or request clarifications in order to accomplish a shared task online. |
| A2 | Can interact online with a supportive partner in a simple collaborative task, responding to basic instructions and seeking clarification, provided there are some visual aids such as images, statistics or graphs to clarify the concepts involved. |
| | Can respond to simple instructions and ask simple questions in order to accomplish a shared task online with the help of a supportive interlocutor. |
| A1 | Can complete a very simple online form, providing basic personal information (such as name, email address or telephone number). |

Source: Adapted from North *et al.* (2018: 99).

## Mediating Concepts

The scales of achievement shown in Tables 13.1 and 13.2 are designed specifically to assess aspects of online communication. Other scales of achievement in the 2018 *Companion* to the *CEFR* are not related specifically to computer-mediated communication, but they are still relevant to the assessment of contributions to online intercultural exchanges. As we observed above, one of the major differences between the 2001 and 2018 descriptors of proficiency lies in the treatment of mediation. Mediation in the *CEFR* includes the 'mediation of concepts' that is, the way that language functions as 'a tool used to think about a subject and to talk about that thinking in a dynamic co-constructive process' (North *et al.*, 2018: 117). The mediation of concepts is seen as a complex process that involves at least two stages: establishing conditions of cooperation by facilitating collaborative interaction with peers, and then developing ideas by collaborating to construct meaning. The 2018 *Companion* presents scales relevant to each stage in this process (Table 13.3).

Unlike the scales shown in Tables 13.1 and 13.2, those reproduced in Table 13.3 assume face-to-face interaction. The achievement scales in Table 13.3 might therefore be used directly to assess participants' performance in a synchronous online event, like a videoconference (see Chapter 11); however, they might also be adapted slightly so that they can be used for asynchronous communication. For example, if we look at the lower level of B1 performance, the facilitative stage can be reworked as 'Can invite other people in a group to respond or participate', while the development stage can be conceptualised as 'Can repeat back part of what someone has posted to confirm mutual understanding and help keep the development of ideas on course'. The scales for 'collaborating to construct meaning' are particularly useful for reflecting in-class about the kind of behaviour that would lend itself to the development of more extensive discussion threads online.

In short, those achievement scales included in the *CEFR* and the later *Companion* that might not seem at first sight relevant to telecollaboration can still prove useful as instruments of assessment, with some minor changes. This is particularly true of those scales in the *Companion* that address mediation.

## Exemplars

To conclude this chapter, it is useful to consider how particular examples of participant interaction might be assessed according to one of the scales shown above. The posts in Figures 13.1 and 13.2 are considered with respect to the scale related to online conversation and discussion (i.e. Table 13.1).

Using the scale of reference for 'Online conversation and discussion' (Table 13.1), Participant 1's contribution might be assessed at the A2 level: 'Can make short descriptive online postings about everyday matters, social activities and feelings, with simple key details'. Both participants introduce themselves with reference to their full name and nickname, and follow the general guidelines suggested by the organiser's prompts. Participant 1's posting is short and descriptive, and touches

**Table 13.3**   Mediating concepts

| Facilitating collaborative interaction with peers | Collaborating to construct meaning |
|---|---|
| **C2** | *No descriptor available* | Can summarise, evaluate and link the various contributions in order to facilitate agreement for a solution or way forward. |
| **C1** | Can show sensitivity to different perspectives within a group, acknowledging contributions and formulating any reservations, disagreements or criticisms in such a way as to avoid or minimise any offence.<br><br>Can develop the interaction and tactfully help steer it towards a conclusion. | Can frame a discussion to decide a course of action with a partner or group, reporting on what others have said, summarising, elaborating and weighing up multiple points of view.<br><br>Can evaluate problems, challenges and proposals in a collaborative discussion in order to decide the way forward.<br><br>Can highlight inconsistencies in thinking, and challenge others' ideas in the process of trying to reach a consensus. |
| **B2** | Can, based on people's reactions, adjust the way he/she formulates questions and/or intervenes in a group interaction. Can act as rapporteur in a group discussion, noting ideas and decisions, discussing these with the group and later giving a summary of the group's view(s) in a plenary. | Can highlight the main issue that needs to be resolved in a complex task and the important aspects that need to be taken into account.<br><br>Can contribute to collaborative decision-making and problem-solving, expressing and co-developing ideas, explaining details and making suggestions for future action.<br><br>Can help organise the discussion in a group by reporting what others have said, summarising, elaborating and weighing up different points of view. |
| | Can ask questions to stimulate discussion on how to organise collaborative work. Can help to define goals for teamwork and compare options for how to achieve them. Can refocus a discussion by suggesting what to consider next, and how to proceed. | Can further develop other people's ideas and opinions.<br><br>Can present his/her ideas in a group and pose questions that invite reactions from other group members' perspectives.<br><br>Can consider two different sides of an issue, giving arguments for and against, and propose a solution or compromise. |
| **B1** | Can collaborate on a shared task, for example formulating and responding to suggestions, asking whether people agree, and proposing alternative approaches.<br><br>Can collaborate on simple, shared tasks and work towards a common goal in a group by asking and answering straightforward questions.<br><br>Can define the task in basic terms in a discussion and ask others to contribute their expertise and experience. | Can organise the work in a straightforward collaborative task by stating the aim and explaining in a simple manner the main issue that needs to be resolved.<br><br>Can use questions, comments and simple reformulations to maintain the focus of a discussion. |
| | Can invite other people in a group to speak. | Can ask a group member to give the reason(s) for their views.<br><br>Can repeat back part of what someone has said to confirm mutual understanding and help keep the development of ideas on course. |

*(Continued)*

**Table 13.3**  (Continued)

| Facilitating collaborative interaction with peers | Collaborating to construct meaning |
|---|---|
| A2 | Can collaborate on simple, shared tasks, provided that other participants speak slowly and that one or more of them help him/her to contribute and to express his/her suggestions. | Can ensure that the person he/she is talking to understands what he/she means by asking appropriate questions. |
| | Can collaborate on simple, practical tasks, asking what others think, making suggestions and understanding responses, provided he/she can ask for repetition or reformulation from time to time. | Can make simple remarks and pose occasional questions to indicate that he/she is following.<br><br>Can make suggestions in a simple way in order to move the discussion forward. |
| A1 | Can invite others' contributions to very simple tasks using short, simple phrases. Can indicate that he/she understands and ask whether others understand. | Can express an idea with very simple words and ask what others think. |
| Pre-A1 | *No descriptors available* | *No descriptors available* |

Source: North *et al.* (2018: 119).

---

Participant 1 (Israel)

hi everyone my name is [*full name*] , and my family call me [*nickname*], I'm 22 ears old and I'm a forth year student at the Arab Academic college of education in Haifa, I study English because I loved English since I was young.

I love to read, journal and to embroidery.

winter is my favorite season because I love cold weather and the rain.

I would like to travel to London.

Participant 2 (Brazil)

Hi guys!

My name is [*full name*], but you can call me [*nickname*] or [*nickname*], all of my friends and family call me like that. I'm 17 years old and I live in a sunny city called Natal, in north-west of Brazil.

In my free time I have ballet/jazz/hiphop classes, I Love dancing, makes me feel free! I Also like to Watch Tv series and I am a big fan of brazilian music (we have a lot of rhythms).

I dont have a specific favourite season, in my city its always summer, but for me its good, I Love January because everybody its in the mood of party and beach !

I am really passionate about discover the world and New cultures, I wanna visit as many places as I can. Italy, Greece, Egipt, hawaii, mexico, Peru, thailand... :D

---

**Figure 13.1** Introductions

on everyday matters without fully engaging the reader. There are some issues with regard to linguistic accuracy, though it is debatable whether an online post demands a high degree of accuracy with respect to the conventions of written standard English – conventions of punctuation, for example, are more flexible than they would be in a formal essay. However, there are grammatical errors such as the confusion between noun and verb in 'to embroidery' (sic).

Participant 3 (Israel)

What concerns me is everything related to the environment; global warming, acid rain, air pollution, urban sprawl, waste disposal, ozone layer depletion, water pollution, climate change. Because all of these problems are related to each other. To deal with these issues in my community as a future teacher, I would like to raise awareness in schools about the importance of the environment, the impacts of a healthy and unhealthy nature and then I would like to present different pictures that show the pollution and the environmental problems and ask students to bring examples from their personal lives and the surroundings, I would like also to have field classes where students need to go out in nature and clean it, then I would provide techniques and methods and ways that help to heal nature.

In addition to this concern, I would like to shed the light on the issue of equality, discrimination, and crimes; killing and shooting.

-How can international connections such as the one we have right here help?

International connections might be a good place to present and discuss these topics, and they might help in healing them as well, where we can share different alternatives and methods that decrease pollution, and different people from different countries can share their experiences and we can learn from each other. But the problem is that the issue of environmental problems is considered a political issue among some.

I hope the next generations will make changes and help with building a better world to live in.

STAY SAFE.

Participant 4 (Brazil)

Like many of you said, one of the biggest concerns about the world nowadays is climate change.

It's known that we must change our behaviors in order to save our planet, but I feel that every good change is taking too long to happen worldwide, for example, renewable energy, green vehicles, and biodegradable plastic. It's really sad to see the amount of trash and pollution we release to the environment.

I live in the Northeast of Brazil, where lots of areas are already in desertification process. This is very scary, it seems that the next Earth extinction is coming and we humans are speeding abruptly the process.

Preservation, reforestation, and a reduction in carbon emissions are urgent and should be priorities to any Government. I believe it is important to discuss these topics in society but also to require from companies and the Government significative reduction in pollution and specialized institutions to support recycling, clean energy, and proper waste disposal and treatment.

**Figure 13.2** Online discussions

In comparison, Participant 2, while following the same overall pattern, might be judged to be at the B2 level: 'Can participate actively in an online discussion, stating and responding to opinions on topics of interest at some length, provided contributors avoid unusual or complex language and allow time for responses'. The length of Participant 2's response is fuller and, while the language remains conventional it invites readers to have some kind of affective response (e.g. 'I live in a sunny city called Natal') and the author provides extra details, sometimes in parenthetical comments (e.g. 'we have lots of rhythms'). Although there is non-conventional capitalising, the linguistic accuracy of the post is also at a higher level than that of Participant 1, and Participant 2 also seeks to engage readers through punctuation ('!') and the use of emojis.

The performance level of both participants is constrained by the nature of the prompt – there is obviously only so much that can be done with a self-introduction. To assess the competences of the participants more fully, the organisers would have to look at the frequency and range of their later contributions to a number of online tasks. The two posts shown in Figure 13.2 are part of a longer thread by various participants in response to a prompt probing the group's views on global citizenship and the problems facing the world.

Participant 3's post has a range of vocabulary and a level of linguistic accuracy that would warrant a B2 assessment according to the scales shown in Table 13.1: she clearly signals her concerns, expresses them fully and engages the readers by asking and answering a rhetorical question that addresses the group as a whole. She employs capitals for emphasis at the end of her post, thus displaying awareness of some of the conventions associated with online communication. To progress to a C1/C2 level, however, according to the *CEFR* descriptors, she would be expected to reproduce this level of sophistication in a synchronous interaction.

Participant 4 also shows a good B2 level of performance, i.e. 'Can engage in online exchanges, linking his/her contributions to previous ones in the thread ["like many of you said"], understanding cultural implications and reacting appropriately ["This is very scary"]'. Again, to move up this scale of achievement, the participant would need to be given the opportunity to interact synchronously with other members of the community. Alternatively, the scales would need to be rewritten with a view to describing the C1/C2 levels of performance in asynchronous interactions.

## Conclusion

This chapter has suggested how some of the descriptors presented in the 2018 *Companion* to the *CEFR* (North *et al.*, 2018) might be adapted and applied to online intercultural exchanges. Other scales of achievement in this extensive set of guidelines might also be relevant to some exchanges, e.g. there is a useful scale of achievement for 'interviewing and being interviewed' (North *et al.*, 2018: 91). However, there are sets of assumptions embedded in each of the scales that organisers of online intercultural exchanges need to be aware of, such as the presupposition that a C level online discussion will likely be synchronous rather than asynchronous. The organisers and instructors of online intercultural exchanges will need to critically consider their assessment instruments, to ensure that they are fit for their own particular purposes.

# 14 Evaluating an Online Intercultural Exchange

At the conclusion of a telecollaboration, organisers and instructors may wish to conduct a formal or informal evaluation of the exchange, or an 'impact study'. There are numerous reasons for doing so. Organisers and instructors might simply seek evidence that the exchange has achieved the intended outcomes agreed at the start of the telecollaboration (Chapter 4) in order to modify and improve future editions. An informal evaluation can help organisers and instructors rethink their goals and the means of achieving them. A formal evaluation can also provide institutions or sponsors with evidence of the effectiveness of the telecollaboration. It is also one of the main sources of evidence for action research (Chapter 15) that can inform the broader educational community of best practices.

Recent years have seen an increase in the number of formal evaluations, or impact studies, of telecollaborations published (O'Dowd, 2021: 8). Online intercultural exchanges have now been practiced for more than a quarter of a century and, consequently, educators are interested in determining whether or not they have had a positive effect on learning. This chapter draws on the published studies and our own experience to give some advice on how to undertake an impact study – formally or informally – on a small scale. The chapter covers the aims of the impact study, quantitative and qualitative research instruments, collecting and analysing data and acting on the findings.

## Aims of the Evaluation

Not every evaluation is identical. When reviewing a telecollaboration, organisers and instructors may wish to focus on different aspects of it: Did participants enhance their intercultural communicative competence (ICC)? Did instructors feel confident with the technical aspects of the telecollaboration? Were participants and instructors satisfied or not with the experience of the exchange? Not every evaluation will necessarily cover all of these aspects, nor cover them to a similar degree or in similar ways. The first step is for the evaluators to decide what exactly they wish to evaluate, and then collect and analyse data in a reliable fashion. There are various instruments that will help them to do this. Usually, these instruments are classified as quantitative or qualitative. We illustrate the two types in turn.

## Quantitative Instruments

Quantitative instruments provide items of data that can be counted and then subjected to statistical analysis. They include surveys that have multiple-choice responses or responses on a numerical scale, usually 1 to 5 (i.e. a Likert scale). Surveys of this kind are generally easy to administer and can be distributed online. Such surveys can be designed to measure participant satisfaction with the exchange, or ICC, or other forms of linguistic or technical competence.

Reliable survey questions are difficult to construct. Those who are new to an impact evaluation might adopt or adapt a model that has been used in earlier surveys. One comprehensive report into instructors' experiences of virtual online exchanges (The EVALUATE Group, 2019) used several surveys to gauge participants' satisfaction, instructors' technical competence and the effect on participants' ICC. Figure 14.1 illustrates a simple set of questions that can be used to measure participants' satisfaction with the course.

This kind of survey can be administered online using polling software, although, as with the choice of an online platform, organisers should check that the software works in all the regions that are to be surveyed.

A more extensive survey can be used in an attempt to gauge the impact of an exchange on participants' ICC. There are different ways of attempting to assess ICC. The EVALUATE Group (2019) adopted a 20-item survey based on an instrument designed by Portalla and Chen (2010) to measure an individual's ability to achieve communicative goals during intercultural interaction. This assessment of 'intercultural effectiveness' groups the 20 items into general categories (cf. Chen, 2007; Portalla & Chen, 2010: 23–28; The EVALUATE Group, 2019):

- Behavioural flexibility: The ability to monitor interactions and contribute with behaviour appropriate to the given situational context.

---

On a scale of 1 to 5, indicate how much you agree with the following statements. (1 = disagree strongly, 2 = disagree, 3 = no opinion, 4 = agree, 5 = agree strongly)

a. I learned a lot from this online intercultural exchange.

b. The online exchange helped me improve my language skills.

c. The online exchange improved my understanding of other cultures.

d. I would recommend this kind of exchange to my friends.

e. This kind of exchange should be included in all language courses.

---

**Figure 14.1**   Possible questionnaire items to measure satisfaction

- Interaction relaxation: The ability to contribute to interactions with others without anxiety or apprehension.
- Interaction management: The ability to initiate and contribute to turn-taking; to contribute to question–answer and interviewing situations, etc.
- Message skills: The ability to express oneself clearly and precisely using the verbal and non-verbal communicative resources available, and to understand the responses proficiently.
- Identity maintenance: The ability to attend to the other's cultural identity and to preserve their face during interactions.
- Interactant respect: The ability to establish and maintain rapport (see Chapter 8) and to recognise that effective communication depends on mutual collaboration.

Figure 14.2 shows a set of 20 survey questions designed by Portalla and Chen (2010: 36) to measure participants' competences in the above areas. As some of the items refer to face-to-face interactions, they need to be sampled from or adapted for online intercultural exchanges. The EVALUATE Group (2019), for example, administered their adapted 20-item survey to an experimental group and a control group before their exchange was run. The experimental group then participated in the online exchange, while the control group did not. After the exchange, the survey was administered to each group again and the results compared.

The advantage of a quantitative survey like this is that the results can be collated and subjected to statistical tests of reliability. The disadvantages are also clear: the data depends on self-reporting and, even if they report honestly, participants might not be the best judges of their own behaviour or attitudes. Participants might have different understandings of key concepts such as 'respect' in items such as 'I always show respect for the opinions of my culturally different counterparts during our interaction'. Finally, the very concept of 'intercultural communicative effectiveness' is a construct of the researchers and the survey designers. Some important aspects of those qualities and competences that make intercultural communication effective might have been overlooked.

Even so, this kind of quantitative survey is useful for those organisers and instructors who need to provide hard data that the exchange has had some kind of positive impact on the participants' attitudes and behaviour. Once devised, quantitative instruments are easy and quick to administer, and the data collated can be subjected to statistical analysis. The use of statistics may be new to those involved in evaluating telecollaborations; Woodrow (2014) is a useful introduction to inferential statistics for applied linguists.

In short, quantitative instruments can give evaluators useful, basic information relatively easily. To dig deeper, though, evaluators might wish to adopt qualitative as well as quantitative instruments of evaluation.

On a scale of 1 to 5, indicate how much you agree with the following statements. (1 = disagree strongly, 2 = disagree, 3 = no opinion, 4 = agree, 5 = agree strongly)

1. I find it is easy to talk with people from different cultures.
2. I am afraid to express myself when interacting with people from different cultures.
3. I find it is easy to get along with people from different cultures.
4. I am not always the person I appear to be when interacting with people from different cultures.
5. I am able to express my ideas clearly when interacting with people from different cultures.
6. I have problems with grammar when interacting with people from different cultures.
7. I am able to answer questions effectively when interacting with people from different cultures.
8. I find it is difficult to feel my culturally different counterparts are similar to me.
9. I use appropriate eye contact when interacting with people from different cultures.
10. I have problems distinguishing between informative and persuasive messages when interacting with people from different cultures.
11. I always know how to initiate a conversation when interacting with people from different cultures.
12. I often miss parts of what is going on when interacting with people from different cultures.
13. I feel relaxed when interacting with people from different cultures.
14. I often act like a very different person when interacting with people from different cultures.
15. I always show respect for my culturally different counterparts during our interaction.
16. I always feel a sense of distance with my culturally different counterparts during our interaction.
17. I find I have a lot in common with my culturally different counterparts during our interaction.
18. I find the best way to act is to be myself when interacting with people from different cultures.
19. I find it is easy to identify with my culturally different counterparts during our interaction.
20. I always show respect for the opinions of my culturally different counterparts during our interaction.

*Behavioural flexibility items are 2, 4, 14 and 18; interaction relaxation items are 1, 3, 11, 13 and 19; interactant respect items are 9, 15 and 20; message skills items are 6, 10 and 12; identity maintenance items are 8, 16 and 17; interaction management items are 5 and 7.*

**Figure 14.2**   Survey of intercultural communicative effectiveness (Portalla & Chen, 2010: 36)

## Qualitative Instruments

Qualitative instruments of evaluation include individual and group interviews, participant and instructor reflective journals and written post-exchange reflective essays. The evaluator can prompt those who are providing the data to different degrees, resulting in, for example, structured, semi-structured and unstructured interviews, journals or essays. In other words, the subjects can be asked to respond to particular topics that the evaluator believes to be important, or they can respond in any way they choose to more general prompts. A more general prompt might be 'Tell me how you felt about the exchange'. A more specific prompt might be based on items in the survey in the previous section, e.g. 'Do you find yourself nervous or relaxed when interacting with people from other cultures? Can you give me an example?'.

The advantage of qualitative instruments when compared to quantitative surveys is that respondents have more opportunities to elaborate on their replies, and important topics might emerge that had not occurred to the evaluators. The disadvantage is, of course, that rich data is messier. Interviews normally need to be recorded or videoed, and then transcribed, in full or in part. It then needs to be analysed. The most common way of analysing qualitative data is to read through it and identify common themes that emerge from the responses. At its most sophisticated, this kind of analysis is known as 'grounded theory' (e.g. Hadley, 2017). More formal evaluations might make use of software, such as Nvivo or Atlas.ti, which has been designed to help organise qualitative data. Such software can help evaluators to organise and code material thematically, and evaluators can run text analysis programs that identify words that are most frequently used by respondents.

The qualitative data collated, its analysis and the resulting findings will obviously be specific to the particular telecollaboration evaluated. While it will be difficult to generalise from the qualitative data to other telecollaborations, the findings will usually be more nuanced than those elicited by quantitative instruments, and they might give rise to new insights and hypotheses that can be tested in future exchanges. For example, the EVALUATE Group (2019: 36–39) discusses responses in learner journals that address aspects of cultural difference. By bringing contributions on this theme together, they classified possible mechanisms for coping with difference as follows:

- Not acknowledging any significant difference ('we are all the same').
- Minimising difference ('our cultures do not differ much').
- Exploring and comparing difference (us versus them).
- Deeper engagement with difference (recognition of cultural relativity).
- Seeing complexity in diversity (theorising cultural difference).

This classification is based on an analysis of a number of responses by participants who do not recognise difference or minimise it; or see difference as marking 'us' versus 'them'; or see attitudes, values and beliefs as relative to differing contexts; or recognise that cultural difference is produced by numerous, complex, dynamic factors (The EVALUATE Group, 2019: 37–38). This insight might then inform future tasks, which can be explicitly designed to prompt participants to notice, account for and reflect on instances of cultural difference.

## Conclusion

Evaluation takes time. The evaluation instruments have to be designed and disseminated, the results collated and analysed and the findings discussed. If qualitative instruments are used, the process usually involves long hours of transcription and coding. Organisers and instructors will therefore probably choose which aspects of their telecollaboration they want, or need, to evaluate in any given edition, and sample from the evaluation instruments at their disposal. Ideally, to increase the reliability of the evaluation, they will triangulate their data by mixing methods, e.g. combining survey data with focus group interviews. This mixing has the advantage of giving both a broad-stroke sense of how participants feel about the exchange, and about the competences they have brought to it, and developed or consolidated during it, and also some deeper insights into aspects of it that interest the evaluators.

Because of the required investment in time, it is relatively rare for organisers and instructors to embark on full-scale, formal evaluations of telecollaborations for the sake of improving the experience for future participants. It is not uncommon, however, for an organiser or instructor who wishes to gain a university degree or to publish a paper in a journal of education or applied linguistics, to develop a more sophisticated evaluation as part of action research on a telecollaboration. The use of a telecollaboration in action research is the topic of our final chapter.

# 15 Developing an Action Research Project

A number of readers of this book will be interested in going beyond the kind of evaluation described in Chapter 14 and treating their telecollaboration as a potential topic for more extensive research. Research on a telecollaboration might be conducted by organisers, instructors or even participants who are pursing graduate studies in education or applied linguistics. Graduate instructors or organisers might be interested in publishing research articles on their work, for career advancement. Others still might simply be interested in enhancing their pedagogical practices by inquiring into them systematically and seeking new ways of improving them.

Whatever the reasons for conducting research, the process will begin with a review of the burgeoning research literature on telecollaborations, only a fraction of which has been mentioned in this volume. Online intercultural exchanges offer a wealth of potential research questions and the research literature will help clarify them and suggest ways of answering them. For example, research questions pertinent to the present volume include:

- How do we understand interculturality and in what ways might a telecollaboration enhance intercultural communicative competences?
- How do participants co-construct their cultural identities online?
- What aspects of linguistic competence are required and enhanced by an online intercultural exchange?
- What skills do participants bring to mediation online?
- What is the impact of instructors' interventions in online exchanges?

While many of these questions have already been addressed in the research literature (cf. Dooly & O'Dowd, 2018; O'Dowd & Dooly, 2020), the findings of previous researchers can be confirmed, challenged and extended through further research into new telecollaborations.

Whatever the specific research questions the researcher alights upon, inquiries into online intercultural exchanges will generally have the character of *action research*, that is, research grounded in actual pedagogical practices that is aimed at improving those practices. As such, action research tends to go through a limited number of predictable phases that are illustrated in this chapter.

## The Principles of Action Research

Tripp (2005: 444) argues that the methodology of action research requires a family of activities that are involved in a perpetual cycle, as illustrated in Figure 15.1.

Educators who advocate action research voice common concerns: action research is cooperative and involves researchers and subjects in a participatory and collaborative manner (Thiollent, 2011), and the data collected during action research should be analysed with a view to improving good practice (Nunan, 1992; Tripp, 2005; Wallace, 1998). If organisers and instructors intend to use the telecollaboration for research purposes, then that intention should be made clear to their partners at the goal-setting stage of the telecollaboration, and consent for the use of the data for research and publication should be sought from participants (Chapter 4). Researchers also need to be flexible. Since they are dealing with unpredictable interactions that are beyond their direct control, the goals of the research might change as the project develops. It will usually be necessary to review, adapt and even change the research questions periodically as the telecollaboration develops.

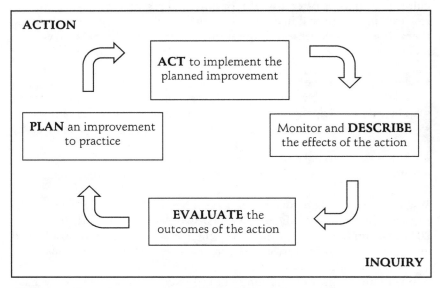

**Figure 15.1** The action research cycle (Tripp, 2005: 444)

Tripp's four-step cycle is divided into two general phases: action and inquiry. The action phase begins with a plan for action, that is, a pedagogical innovation. This might be the establishment of a new online intercultural exchange, or a change in the way an existing telecollaboration is implemented. The plan is then acted on, and the innovation is implemented. The inquiry phase begins with monitoring and describing the effects of the innovation. This can be done via observation, surveys, data collection and interviews. This step gathers and analyses much of the core data for the research. The final step in the cycle is the evaluation of the data (cf. Chapter 14). The evaluation then feeds into planning for further innovations, and the cycle begins again.

The following sections look in closer detail at the two main phases, action and inquiry, and illustrate some ways in which telecollaborations can be used in action research. In doing so, we draw on some of the issues and themes raised earlier in this volume.

## Action: Planning and Implementing an Innovation

An obvious component of planning is mutual goal-setting (see Chapter 4). Tripp (2005: 455) advocates that collaborative action research should deal with topics that are genuinely of mutual interest, and shared goals clearly fall into that category. Tripp also stresses the importance of shared commitment to the project. The development of the ethos of shared commitment is neither trivial nor easy: it depends on clear communication among partners and transparent mechanisms for active participation. As noted in Chapter 10, problems invariably arise, and there need to be agreed means of alerting partners to them, and joint approaches to dealing with them when they arise. Planning involves organisers, instructors and participants; there may be time before the telecollaboration starts to negotiate content and aims with participants. However, participants' involvement in planning might take the form of an ongoing refinement and extension of the goals and content initially decided by organisers and instructors.

From planning, the action research focus moves to implementation. As we have seen, online intercultural exchanges can be diverse in nature: they can be discussion forums, book or cinema groups, or task oriented. To illustrate the planning and implementation of a telecollaboration used as the basis for a graduate research project, we draw on one online intercultural exchange between students in Brazil and the United States. This telecollaboration pre-dated the widespread use of social media, and used email as the platform for interaction. In this particular telecollaboration, the organisers and instructors in both localities did have time before the interaction started to plan certain aspects with the participating students.

The planning stage fell into two parts: in the first, the instructor explained the nature of the telecollaboration to the students and attempted to raise their interest in interacting with the partner group. At this stage, the Brazilian instructor also assessed students' prior knowledge about and attitude towards the culture represented by the partner group. This data not only fed into the planning of topics, but it also provided benchmark information that could be used later in the description and evaluation of the impact of the course on the participants' knowledge and attitudes. The second part of the planning stage consisted of a set of activities designed to rehearse the interactions with the partner group. Table 15.1 shows a timetable for this stage for the Brazilian group that was involved in the telecollaboration.

In the planning stage, the instructor introduced the project to the Brazilian students who would participate, giving them information about the goals of the project and noting their response, which in this case was a mixture of excitement and apprehension since most of them had never experienced interaction through English with a foreigner, and some lacked confidence in their linguistic skills. The students then went through an intensive rehearsal period during which they studied and prepared for the email interactions by exchanging messages among themselves in English. At this point, some language awareness skills were introduced (cf. Chapter 12).

The rehearsal step reassured students that they would be able to communicate with their partners; it also gave the instructor the opportunity to note what topics they found more and less interesting. It also provided the organisers with input that might circumvent hitherto unanticipated problems; e.g. the Brazilian and American organisers agreed to reschedule the email exchanges so that the Brazilian participants would have more time to compose their messages.

If this stage is going to be used in a formal action research publication (such as a report, thesis or an article), the instructors and organisers

**Table 15.1** The planning stage of a Brazil–US telecollaboration

| Activity | Objective | Amount of hours | Phase according to Tripp's (2005) diagram |
|---|---|---|---|
| Conversation with Brazilian students | Explain the project, the perspectives of contact with international students. | 2 h 25min | Plan |
| Questionnaire | Assess components of intercultural communicative competence (ICC) described by Byram (1997). | 1 h 30 min | Plan/describe/evaluate |
| | Get to know the topics that Brazilian students would be interested in debating with international students. | | |
| Tabulation of questionnaire data | Organisation of the data obtained when applying the tool. | 6 h | |

should keep a record of the interactions among themselves and the participants, their observations and any decisions made. This can be in the form of a teacher's journal or diary.

In the Brazil–US telecollaboration, the organisers were interested in the level of cultural knowledge about the other that each group had at the outset of the project, in order to determine if or how the telecollaboration would impact on participants' cultural awareness and attitudes. They therefore developed a simple questionnaire to survey participants. Two of the questions and findings for this group are shown in Figures 15.2 and 15.3, and a number of 'key words' used by Brazilians to express their presuppositions about Americans are given in Table 15.2.

The findings of these surveys provided the organisers and instructors with useful information. The survey results in Figures 15.2 and 15.3 suggest the sources of the stereotypical aspects of the descriptions given in Table 15.2. It is perhaps sobering to realise that 'school' is reported as

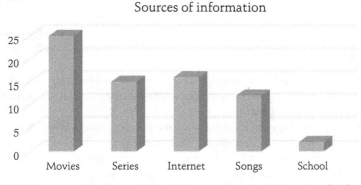

**Figure 15.2** Responses to the question 'What are your main sources of information about the country of your international partners'?

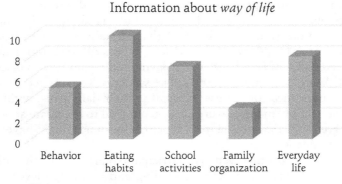

**Figure 15.3** Responses to the question 'What do you think you know about the way of life of the people of this country (i.e. the United States)'?

**Table 15.2** Words used by Brazilian participants to express their ideas about Americans before the telecollaboration started

| | Words used to describe the aspects mentioned |
|---|---|
| Behaviour | Individualists |
| | Consumerists |
| Eating habits | Not healthy |
| | Quite caloric |
| | Very bad |
| | Fast food |
| School activities | Full time |
| | Good teaching |
| | Students can choose subjects |
| | Very significant investment |
| Family organisation | Families are smaller |
| | Americans have few children |
| Everyday life | More organised things |
| | More rules |
| | There is democracy |

being one of the least informative sources about the partner culture, Brazilians' concepts being formed more commonly by popular culture: films, television and social media.

The surveys also provided instructors and organisers with clues about the kinds of topics and discussions that might prove fruitful to explore as the telecollaboration developed, namely, attitudes towards consumerism, diet, family structure and the regulations governing everyday life.

The second step in the preparation with the Brazilian group before the exchange began was to rehearse some of the forms of interaction. Table 15.3 shows in some detail the sequence of preparatory activities used in this rehearsal period. As we have mentioned, given the relative insecurity among this group of Brazilian students about their language proficiency, more time was allocated than initially anticipated to this phase. As Table 15.3 shows, the first activity was to present and analyse the characteristics of email with the class and understand it as a discourse genre (cf. Ware & Kramsch, 2005). The students were invited to reflect on the circumstances of the use of email in their daily lives, within and outside the school, and they were also encouraged to speculate about different perceptions that people from other backgrounds might have about this communication channel.

Activities (2)–(8) involved the participants agreeing on the rules of 'netiquette' (Chapter 5), practicing sending and receiving messages and analysing each other's texts. This rehearsal phase aimed at not only

**Table 15.3** Preparatory activities used with Brazilian participants to rehearse interactions

| Activity | Objective | Amount of hours |
|---|---|---|
| (1) Presentation of email as a discourse genre | Reflect on the circumstances of using email in their daily lives inside and outside of school. | 2 h 25 min |
| (2) 'Do's and Don'ts' in emails – netiquette | Discussing etiquette rules on the internet. | 2 h 25 min |
| (3) Activity: Students send messages to the teacher (various topics) | Practice using this means of communication in the school context. | 2 h 25 min |
| (4) Activity: Projection of the emails sent to the teacher in the classroom (omitting the students' names) | Discuss the degree of formality of the text and ask questions about grammatical topics. | 3 h 55 min |
| (5) Activity: Exchange of messages between students | Practice questions and answers in emails using two different scenarios: (a) communication with an American high school student (more informal context); (b) communication with the principal of an American high school (more formal context). | 2 h 25 min |
| (6) Activity: Projection in the classroom of the emails exchanged by the students | Analyse the messages exchanged by the students dealing with the degree of formality of the texts. | 2 h 25 min |
| (7) Presentation of greetings, farewells and other expressions | Exercise greetings, goodbyes and other expressions for requesting information and clarifying doubts in a 'casually formal' manner. | 45 min |
| (8) Activity: Simulation of situations | List strategies to deal with possible discomforts that are generated by the interaction between cultures or even when stereotypes appear. | 3 h 10 min |
| (9) Activity: Focus on language | Reinforce the grammatical part of the texts based on the most frequent errors observed in the messages written by the students in the preparation phase of the class. | 3 h 10 min |

improving the linguistic level of the text but also training the participants to think interculturally. For an action research project, the instructor should keep a record of the interactions produced at this stage, again as a benchmark against which later interactions can be compared.

## Inquiry: Describing and Evaluating Data

The Brazilian–US exchange described above had an intensive planning and rehearsal stage. The participants in the two locations were subsequently introduced to each other, and they interacted via email, responding to tasks given by the instructors. The instructors continued to compile data as the exchange progressed. Sources of data at this stage included:

- email interactions written by both groups of participants;
- records of ongoing interactions among the instructors/organisers;
- post-exchange surveys of participants' knowledge and attitudes;
- evaluation surveys/interviews.

The email interactions between participants provide a record of progress in the acquisition of intercultural communicative competences. The resulting data can be used in various ways. The participants' performance in the rehearsal phase might be compared with their performance at the end of the exchange, using scales of achievement (Chapter 13). Records of ongoing interactions among the instructors and organisers can provide evidence of shifts in the goals or expectations of the interactions. Post-exchange surveys of knowledge and attitudes can, like the interactions themselves, be compared to those employed in the rehearsal phase, and so provide evidence of the development of participants' intercultural communicative competence and the impact of the exchange on their developing interculturality.

A major part of this phase of the action research cycle will be a full-scale evaluation of the kind described in Chapter 14. Evaluation surveys, diaries and interviews indicate the extent to which the participants and instructors felt that the telecollaboration achieved its stated and agreed goals.

The action researcher needs time and opportunity to gather all the data mentioned above, analyse it and write a report that might take the form of a thesis, journal article or book chapter (e.g. Bitchener, 2009). Recommendations for future improvement can be offered, although such recommendations will be tailored to the intended audience of the report, thesis, article or chapter. Thus, the action research cycle begins again.

## Conclusion

The concluding chapter has sought to give a brief overview of how readers might take an online intercultural exchange as an opportunity to undertake action research, individually or collaboratively. The example given here of the Brazil–US exchange is intended to illustrate how one such exchange became the basis for an action research project that explored the Brazilian participants' developing communicative repertoire and their changing knowledge of and attitude towards Americans as a consequence of their participation in the telecollaboration. The action research was subsequently developed into a successful doctoral project (Lima, 2017).

This particular exchange involved an extensive preparation stage that included surveys of knowledge and attitude. One general research question addressed was whether the exchange affected participants' knowledge and attitude about their partners' culture. Other action research projects might have different study objectives, e.g. they might look at how participants use multimodal resources (text, emojis, gifs, images, sound, video) to develop rapport (Chapter 8) or the relationship between asynchronous and synchronous interaction (Chapter 11). Many of the issues raised in different chapters in this book can themselves inform the questions addressed by action research.

Action research is time-consuming but it can be rewarding. The investment of time may result in a graduate qualification for an individual or bestow on collaborating researchers the reputational boost that follows publication in a scholarly journal or book. More importantly, such an investment can improve the quality of future exchanges and contribute an understanding of good practice to the educational community.

# Afterword

This book has sought to introduce readers to the frustrations and joys of designing, organising, facilitating and researching online intercultural exchanges. Its content is practical rather than theoretical – although we have benefited from the abundance of research literature on online exchanges that now exists, we have relied largely on our direct experience of involvement in such exchanges, to give readers, we hope, a realistic sense of the challenges of setting off down this path. We hope novices will learn from our many mistakes, and that those readers who have already participated in online intercultural exchanges will recognise their own experiences in the foregoing pages, and perhaps find them affirmed and validated.

We have sought not to downplay the frustrations and challenges faced, at times, by organisers, instructors and participants. When we started off ourselves, we perhaps shared an idealistic vision of enthusiastic participants, eagerly interacting in the new virtual universe, taking full advantage of its affordances to engage in intercultural exploration, with minimal interference from instructors. That vision has never quite been realised though it has never fully disappeared. Every online exchange that we have been part of has been a compromise, resulting in a reappraisal of our sense of achievable goals. But each has also been a happy surprise, as the interactions among participants have seldom failed to bring us new insights into intercultural communication – and, indeed, human nature.

Our final message, then, is not to lose heart if your own first attempts at an online intercultural exchange do not go to plan. As one of our early collaborators, Alison Phipps, once observed, during a dark moment for one of the authors of the present book, intercultural communicative competence is essentially about finding imaginative and constructive ways of dealing with mess. No matter how well you design an online exchange in advance, running it will always be an uncertain adventure. We trust the adventure will be as exciting, surprising and enriching for you as it has been for us.

# References

Agar, M. (1994) *Language Shock: Understanding the Culture of Conversation*. New York: Perennial.

Alareer, R., Al-Masri, N., de Lima, B.F. and Weissheimer, J. (2022) Connecting Palestine and Brazil: Towards a critical and creative intercultural pedagogy for online intercultural exchange. In P. Holmes and J. Corbett (eds) *Critical Intercultural Pedagogy for Difficult Times: Conflict, Crisis, and Creativity* (pp. 48–63). New York: Routledge.

Anderson, W. and Corbett, J. (2015) 'What do we chat about when we chat about culture?' The discourse of online intercultural exchanges. In N. Tcherepashenets (ed.) *Globalizing On-line: Telecollaboration, Internationalization and Social Justice* (pp. 177–200). New York: Peter Lang.

Anthony, L. (2021) AntConc (Version 4.0.0) [Computer Software]. Waseda University, Japan. See http://www.antlab.sci.waseda.ac.jp/ (accessed 18 July 2022).

Aranha, S. and Cavalari, S. (2014) A trajetória do projeto Teletandem Brasil: Da modalidade institucional não-integrada à institucional integrada. *The ESPecialist* 35 (2), 70–88.

Aranha, S. and Leone, P. (2017) The development of DOTI (Data of oral teletandem interaction). In D. Fišer and M. Beißwenger (eds) *Investigating Computer-Mediated Communication: Corpus-Based Approaches to Language in the Digital World* (pp. 172–192). Ljubljana: Ljubljana University Press.

Belz, J.A. (2007) The development of intercultural communicative competence in telecollaborative partnerships. In R. O'Dowd (ed.) *Online Intercultural Exchange: An Introduction for Foreign Language Teachers* (pp. 127–166). Clevedon: Multilingual Matters.

Belz, J.A. and Thorne, S. (eds) (2006) *Internet-Mediated Intercultural Foreign Language Education*. Boston, MA: Heinle and Heinle.

Bhabha, H. (1994) *The Location of Culture*. New York: Routledge.

Bitchener, J. (2009) *Writing an Applied Linguistics Thesis or Dissertation: A Guide to Presenting Empirical Research*. London: Bloomsbury.

Blommaert, J. and Rampton, B. (2012) Language and superdiversity. *Max Planck Institute for the Study of Religious and Ethnic Diversity* WP 12-09. https://www.mmg.mpg.de/59855/wp-12-09 (accessed 22 June 2023).

Breen, M. and Littlejohn, A. (eds) (2000) *Classroom Decision-Making: Negotiation and Process Syllabuses in Practice*. Cambridge: Cambridge University Press.

Brumfit, C. (1985) *Language and Literature Teaching: From Practice to Principle*. Oxford: Pergamon.

Byram, M. (1997) *Teaching and Assessing Intercultural Communicative Competence*. Clevedon: Multilingual Matters.

Byram, M. (2008) *From Foreign Language Education to Education for Intercultural Citizenship: Essays and Reflections*. Clevedon: Multilingual Matters.

Byram, M. (2021) *Teaching and Assessing Intercultural Communicative Competence: Revisited* (2nd edn). Bristol: Multilingual Matters.

Byram, M. and Parmenter, L. (eds) (2012) *The Common European Framework of Reference: The Globalisation of Language Education Policy*. Bristol: Multilingual Matters.

Chen, G. (2007) A review of the concept of intercultural effectiveness. In M. Hinner (ed.) *The Influence of Culture in the World of Business* (pp. 95–116). Berlin: Peter Lang.

Cope, B. and Kalantzis, M. (eds) (2000) *Multiliteracies: Literacy Learning and the Design of Social Futures*. New York: Routledge.

Corbett, J. (2003) *An Intercultural Approach to English Language Teaching* (1st edn). Clevedon: Multilingual Matters.

Corbett, J. (2010) *Intercultural Language Activities*. Cambridge: Cambridge University Press.

Corbett, J. (2021) Revisiting mediation: Implications for intercultural language education. *Language and Intercultural Communication* 21 (1), 8–23.

Corbett, J. (2022) *An Intercultural Approach to English Language Teaching* (2nd edn). Bristol: Multilingual Matters.

Corbett, J. and Phipps, A. (2006) Culture, language and technological control: Virtual intercultural connections. In G. Linke (ed.) *New Media – New Teaching Options* (pp. 157–178). Heidelberg: Universitätsverlag Winter.

Council of Europe (2001) *Common European Framework of Reference for Languages: Learning, Teaching, Assessment*. Strasbourg: Council of Europe. See https://www.coe.int/en/web/common-european-framework-reference-languages (accessed 22 June 2023).

Dart, H. (2015) The Rio-Warsaw connection: Encouraging interculturalism among students. *English Teaching Forum* 53 (3), 22–29.

Deardoff, D. (ed.) (2009) *The SAGE Handbook of Intercultural Competence*. Thousand Oaks, CA: Sage.

Dervin, F. (2012) Cultural identity, representation and othering. In J. Jackson (ed.) *The Routledge Handbook of Language and Intercultural Communication* (1st edn, pp. 181–194). New York: Routledge.

Dervin, F. (2013) International sociodigital interaction. In F. Sharafian and M. Jamarani (eds) *Language and Intercultural Communication in the New Era* (pp. 83–97). New York: Routledge.

Dervin, F. and Gross, Z. (eds) (2016) *Intercultural Competence in Education: Alternative Approaches for Different Times*. Heidelberg: Springer.

Dooly, M. and O'Dowd, R. (eds) (2018) *In this Together: Teachers' Experiences with Transnational, Telecollaborative Language Learning Projects*. New York: Peter Lang.

Ellis, R. (1991) *Second Language Acquisition and Language Pedagogy*. Clevedon: Multilingual Matters.

Ellis, R. (1993) Second language acquisition and the structural syllabus. *TESOL Quarterly* 27, 91–113.

Ellis, R. (2008) Explicit form-focused instruction and second language acquisition. In B. Spolsky and F. Hult (eds) *The Handbook of Educational Linguistics* (pp. 437–455). Oxford: Blackwell.

Fulcher, G. (2015) *Re-Examining Language Testing*. New York: Routledge.

Garcia, D.N.M. (2012) Ensino/Aprendizagem de línguas em teletandem: Espaços para autonomia e reflexão. *Estudos Linguísticos* 41 (2), 481–494.

Geertz, C. (1986) *The Uses of Diversity*. Ann Arbor, MI: University of Michigan Press.

Guilherme, M.M. (2002) *Critical Citizens for an Intercultural World: Foreign Language Education as Cultural Politics*. Clevedon: Multilingual Matters.

Hadley, G. (2017) *Grounded Theory in Applied Linguistics Research: A Practical Guide*. New York: Routledge.

Ham, J. (1995) Cultural encounters: German and American students meet on the Internet. In M. Warschauer (ed.) *Virtual Connections: Online Activities & Projects for Networking Language Learners* (pp. 107–108). Honolulu, HI: University of Hawai'i at Mānoa.

Harmer, J. (2013) Shall we kill off the digital native? See https://jeremyharmer.wordpress.com/2013/11/22/shall-we-kill-off-the-digital-native (accessed 16 July 2022).

Kramsch, C. and Uryu, M. (2020) Intercultural contact, hybridity and third space. In J. Jackson (ed.) *The Routledge Handbook of Language and Intercultural Communication* (2nd edn, pp. 204–217). New York: Routledge.

Liddicoat, A. and Scarino, A. (2020) Assessing intercultural language learning. In J. Jackson (ed.) *The Routledge Handbook of Language and Intercultural Communication* (2nd edn, pp. 395–407). New York: Routledge.

Lima, B. (2017) Experiência intercultural mediada pela internet: O ensino de língua via telecolaboraçao. PhD thesis, Universidade Federal Rio Grande do Norte, Natal. See https://repositorio.ufrn.br/bitstream/123456789/23491/1/BrunoFerreiraDeLima_TESE.pdf (accessed 22 June 2023).

Lima, B. and Dart, H. (2019) The hemispheres connection. In P. Romanowski and E. Bandura (eds) *Intercultural Foreign Language Teaching and Learning in Higher Education Contexts* (pp. 162–176). Hershey, PA: IGI Global.

Little, D. (2004) Constructing a theory of learner autonomy: Some steps along the way. In K. Mäkinen, P. Kaikkonen and V. Kohonen (eds) *Future Perspectives in Foreign Language Education* (pp. 15–25). Oulu: Oulun Yliopiston kasvatustieteiden tiedekunnan tutkimuksia.

Melchor-Couto, S. and Herrera, B. (2023) Immersive virtual reality: Exploring possibilities for virtual exchange. In A. Anthippi Potolia and M. Derivry-Plard (eds) *Virtual Exchange for Intercultural Language Learning and Teaching: Fostering Communication for the Digital Age*. New York: Routledge.

Menard-Warwick, J., Heredia-Herrera, A. and Palmer, D.S. (2013) Local and global identities in an EFL internet chat exchange. *The Modern Language Journal* 97 (4), 965–980.

Müller-Hartmann, A. (2000) The role of tasks in promoting intercultural learning in electronic learning networks. *Language Learning & Technology* 4 (2), 129–147.

NCSSFL-ACTFL (2017a) What are the NCSSFL-ACTFL can do statements? See https://www.actfl.org/educator-resources/ncssfl-actfl-can-do-statements#0 (accessed 22 June 2023).

NCSSFL-ACTFL (2017b) NCSSFL-ACTFL can-do statements: Performance indicators for language learners. See https://www.actfl.org/educator-resources/ncssfl-actfl-can-do-statements#0"https://www.actfl.org/educator-resources/ncssfl-actfl-can-do-statements#0 (accessed 22 June 2023).

North, B., Goodier, T. and Piccardo, E. (2018) *Common European Framework of Reference for Languages: Learning, Teaching, Assessment: Companion Volume with New Descriptors*. Strasbourg: Council of Europe. See https://www.coe.int/en/web/common-european-framework-reference-languages (accessed 22 June 2023).

Nunan, D. (1989) *Designing Tasks for the Communicative Classroom*. Cambridge: Cambridge University Press.

Nunan, D. (1992) *Research Methods in Language Learning*. Cambridge: Cambridge University Press.

Nunan, D. (2004) *Task-Based Language Teaching*. Cambridge: Cambridge University Press.

O'Dowd, R. (2003) Understanding the 'other side': Intercultural learning in a Spanish-English e-mail exchange. *Language Learning & Technology* 7 (2), 118–144.

O'Dowd, R. (ed.) (2007) *Online Intercultural Exchange: An Introduction for Foreign Language Teachers*. Clevedon: Multilingual Matters.

O'Dowd, R. (2012) Intercultural communicative competence through telecollaboration. In J. Jackson (ed.) *The Routledge Handbook of Language and Intercultural Communication* (1st edn, pp. 340–356). New York: Routledge.

O'Dowd, R. (2021) Virtual exchange: Moving forward into the next decade. *Computer Assisted Language Learning* 34 (3), 1–17. https://doi.org/10.1080/09588221.2021.1902201

O'Dowd, R. and Lewis, T. (eds) (2016) *Online Intercultural Exchange: Policy, Pedagogy, Practice*. New York: Routledge.

O'Dowd, R. and Dooly, M. (2020) Intercultural communicative competence development through telecollaboration and virtual exchange. In J. Jackson (ed.) *The Routledge Handbook of Language and Intercultural Communication* (2nd edn, pp. 361–374). New York: Routledge.

Paine, D.R., Jankowski, P.J. and Sandage, S.J. (2016) Humility as a predictor of intercultural competence: Mediator effects for differentiation-of-self. *The Family Journal* 24 (1), 15–22.

Pohl, U. (2020) Fish is fish: Making the most of a story with a twist. *Humanising Language Teaching* 22 (6). See https://www.hltmag.co.uk/dec20/fish-is-fish (accessed 11 July 2022).

Pohl, U. and Szesztay, M. (2015) Bringing creative, critical and compassionate thinking into ELT. *Humanising Language Teaching* 17 (2). See http://old.hltmag.co.uk/apr15/sart06.htm (accessed 11 July 2022).

Portalla, T. and Chen, G. (2010) The development and validation of the intercultural effectiveness scale. *Intercultural Communication Studies* 19 (3), 21–37. See https://web.uri.edu/iaics/files/02TamraPortallaGuo-MingChen.pdf (accessed 28 July 2022).

Potolia, A. and Derivry-Plard, M. (eds) (2023) *Virtual Exchange for Intercultural Language Learning and Teaching: Fostering Communication for the Digital Age*. New York: Routledge.

Prensky, M. (2001) Digital natives, digital immigrants. *On the Horizon* 9 (5), 1–6. See https://www.marcprensky.com/writing/Prensky%20-%20Digital%20Natives,%20Digital%20Immigrants%20-%20Part1.pdf (accessed 22 June 2023).

Prince, T. (2016) Activities that affect attitude. Paper presented at *NILE@21: Transforming Teaching*, 12–14 August, Norwich.

Redstone, I. (2022) The crisis of moral legitimacy. *Tablet*, 10 January. See https://www.tabletmag.com/sections/news/articles/crisis-moral-legitimacy?campaign_id=229&emc=edit_jm_20220506&instance_id=60698 (accessed 11 July 2022).

Ribbe, E. and Bezanilla, M. (2013) Scaffolding learner autonomy in online university course. *Digital Education Review* 24, 98–113. See https://revistes.ub.edu/index.php/der/article/view/11279 (accessed 15 July 2022).

Richards, K. (2006) 'Being the teacher': Identity and classroom conversation. *Applied Linguistics* 27 (1), 51–77.

Ridings, C., Gefen, D. and Arinze, B. (2006) Psychological barriers: Lurker and poster motivation and behavior in online communities. *Communications of the Association for Information Systems* 18, 329–354.

Risager, K. (2007) *Language and Culture Pedagogy: From a National to a Transnational Paradigm*. Clevedon: Multilingual Matters.

Roberts, C., Byram, M., Barro, A., Jordan, S. and Street, B.V. (2001) *Language Learners as Ethnographers*. Clevedon: Multilingual Matters.

Rojas Giraldo, P. (2021) Icebreakers' implementation in the EFL classroom and their effect on group cohesion in a level 3 English course at Autónoma University during the second semester of 2018. MA Thesis, Universidad del Valle, School of Language Sciences, Santiago de Cali. See https://bibliotecadigital.univalle.edu.co/handle/10893/21557 (accessed 13 July 2022).

Rutherford, W. (1987) *Second Language Grammar: Learning and Teaching*. London: Longman.

Scott, M. (2020) WordSmith Tools (Version 8) [Software]. Stroud: Lexical Analysis Software. See https://lexically.net/wordsmith/ (accessed 18 July 2022).

Souza, R.A. (2003) Telecolaboração e divergência em uma experiência de aprendizagem de português e inglês como línguas estrangeiras. *Revista Brasileira de Linguística Aplicada* 3 (2), 73–96.

Susser, B. (1994) Process approaches in ESL/EFL writing instruction. *Journal of Second Language Writing* 3 (1), 31–47. See https://www.sciencedirect.com/science/article/abs/pii/1060374394900043 (accessed 15 July 2022).

The EVALUATE Group (2019) *Evaluating the Impact of Virtual Exchange on Initial Teacher Education: A European Policy Experiment*. Research-publishing.net. https://doi.org/10.14705/rpnet.2019.29.9782490057337.

Thiollent, M. (2011) Action research and participatory research: An overview. *International Journal of Action Research* 7 (2), 160–174. See https://www.ssoar.info/ssoar/bitstream/handle/document/41407/ssoar-ijar-2011-2-thiollent-Action_Research_and_Participatory_Research.pdf?sequence=1&isAllowed=y&lnkname=ssoar-ijar-2011-2-thiollent-Action_Research_and_Participatory_Research.pdf"https://www.ssoar.info/ssoar/bitstream/handle/document/41407/ssoar-ijar-2011-2-thiollent-Action_Research_and_Participatory_Research.pdf?sequence=1&isAllowed=y&lnkname=ssoar-ijar-2011-2-thiollent-Action_Research_and_Participatory_Research.pdf (accessed 22 June 2023).

Tomaél, M.I. and Marteleto, R.M. (2006) Redes sociais: Posições dos atores no fluxo da informação. *Encontros Bibli: Revista eletrônica De Biblioteconomia E Ciência Da informação* 11 (1), 75–91. https://doi.org/10.5007/1518-2924.2006v11nesp1p75.

Tripp, D. (2005) Action research: A methodological introduction. *Educação e pesquisa* 31, 443–466. See https://www.scielo.br/j/ep/a/3DkbXnqBQqyq5bV4TCL9NSH/?format=pdf&lang=en (accessed 19 July 2022).

Ushioda, E. (2011) Language learning motiviation, self and identity: Current theoretical perspectives. *Computer Assisted Language Learning* 24 (3), 199–210.

Vygotsky, L. (1934) *Thought and Language* (trans. E. Hanfmann and G. Vakar). Cambridge, MA: MIT Press.

Wallace, M. (1998) *Action Research for Language Teachers*. Cambridge: Cambridge University Press.

Ware, P. (2005) 'Missed' communication in online communication: Tensions in a German-American telecollaboration. *Language Learning & Technology* 9 (2), 64–89.

Ware, P.D. and Kramsch, C. (2005) Toward an intercultural stance: Teaching German and English through telecollaboration. *The Modern Language Journal* 89 (2), 190–205.

Warschauer, M. (ed.) (1995) *Virtual Connections: Online Activities & Projects for Networking Language Learners*. Honolulu, HI: University of Hawai'i at Mānoa.

Willis, J. (1996) *A Framework for Task-Based Learning*. Harlow: Longman.

Woodrow, L. (2014) *Writing About Quantitative Research in Applied Linguistics*. Houndmills: Palgrave Macmillan.

Wright, T. and Bolitho, R. (1993) Language awareness: A missing link in language teacher education? *ELT Journal* 47 (4), 292–304.

Zimmerman, D. (1998) Discoursal identities and social identities. In C. Antaki and S. Widdiecombe (eds) *Identities in Talk* (pp. 87–106). London: Sage.

# Index